SO-AXZ-752

SCENERY
FOR MODEL RAILROADS

BY BILL McCLANAHAN

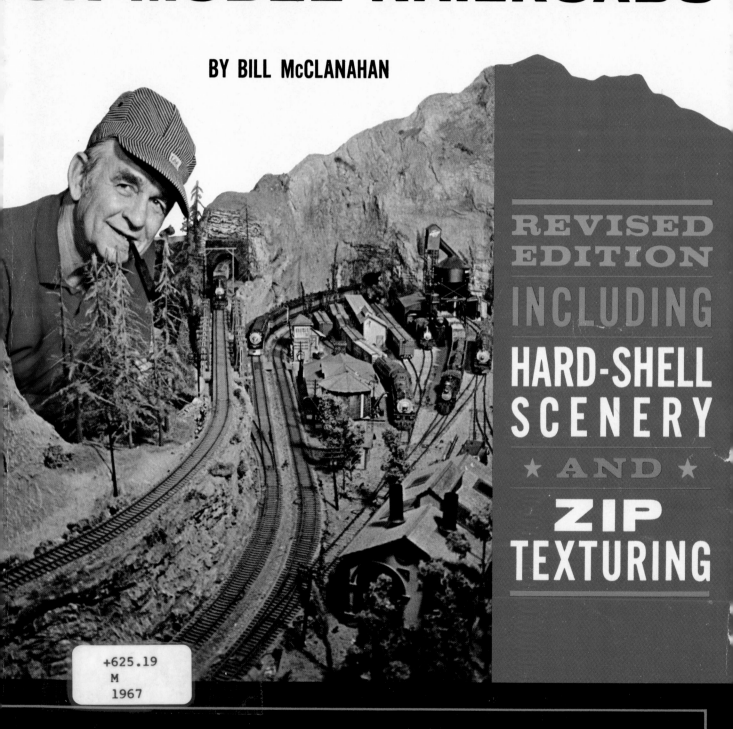

REVISED EDITION

INCLUDING

HARD-SHELL SCENERY

★ **AND** ★

ZIP TEXTURING

+625.19
M
1967

HOW THE EXPERTS DO IT
MADE EASY FOR BEGINNERS

SCENERY
FOR MODEL RAILROADS

BY BILL McCLANAHAN

With chapters by Linn H. Westcott

Wash drawings by Gil Reid

Cover: A scene photographed by Cliff Grant on Bill McClanahan's Texas & Rio Grande Western. Author is in the picture.

Frontispiece: Other photos in chapter 6 show how zip texturing developed this scene on Linn Westcott's model railroad.

KALMBACH BOOKS

© 1958 and 1967 by Kalmbach Publishing Co. All rights reserved. This book may not be reproduced in part or in whole without written permission from the publisher, except in the case of brief quotations used in reviews. Published by Kalmbach Publishing Co., 1027 North Seventh Street, Milwaukee, WI 53233. Printed in U. S. A. Library of Congress Catalog Card Number 67-14545. ISBN: 0-89024-508-8.

FIRST EDITION, 1958. Second printing, 1959. Third printing, 1961. Fourth printing, 1964. SECOND EDITION, 1967. Second printing, 1968. Third printing, 1969. Fourth printing, 1971. Fifth printing, 1972. Sixth printing, 1973. Seventh printing, 1974. Eighth printing, 1975. Ninth printing, 1976. Tenth printing, 1978. Eleventh printing, 1981. Twelfth printing, 1982. Thirteenth printing, 1986. Fourteenth printing, 1988.

1 WHY SCENERY?

A MODEL RAILROAD without scenery is like a locomotive that is minus its cab and boiler — it may operate, but it certainly doesn't look like the real thing. When the railroader first starts in the hobby, he is so thrilled by the sight of his latest locomotive moving a string of cars over his track that it really doesn't take much imagination to envision the supporting realistic scene. In the early enthusiasm of the hobby, that oval of track and its few switches fastened down to a bare slab of material becomes a twisting road of rails winding through colorful ravines and hills, across rivers and into dark, dank tunnels, something like the dream envisioned in fig. 1-1.

However, after a while, as the railroader becomes more sophisticated and the first thrill of seeing something he has actually assembled with his hands move under its own power has faded away, that imaginative prop gives way. For the first time the railroader sees his layout for what it is — a maze of trackage winding its uninteresting way across a tabletop, or the simple oval shown in fig. 1-2.

That point for many railroaders is the crossroads of the hobby. Some continue along the uninteresting way of a barren layout. As they do, they find the hobby less and less fascinating until they reach the point where they are actually bored with the whole thing. Many model railroaders are lost that way. Others, realizing that something is amiss, turn to scenery. When they do, they realize that an entirely new facet of model railroading has been opened to them. To many, it becomes the most fascinating part of the hobby.

Now it has often been said that the tastiness of a meal depends upon the way it is served. This old saw certainly applies to model railroading. That Berkshire locomotive, for which you have just plunked down 70 iron men, certainly looks more like the real thing as it crawls through a background of realistic scenery than it did chuffing across a bare slab of plywood.

The sight of a superdetailed locomotive dragging a string of colorful reefers through a cut and across a spidery trestle, then plunging into the forbidding darkness of a tunnel that bores into a tree- and shrub-crested mountain, fires the imagination and whets the appetite for more and more railroading. The railroader who follows this course continues to get a great kick out of the unending pleasures of this, the most fascinating of all hobbies.

Scenery is the one thing that can differ greatly from layout to layout. It gives the creative railroader his greatest opportunity to express his own individuality. You may visit several dozen model railroads and find that the rolling stock and structures are all the same on each one — but it is doubtful that in the entire nation you will find any two railroads that have their scenery exactly alike.

The reason for this is simple. As the railroader progresses into the building of scenery, he develops a technique of his own — just as an artist develops his technique in putting colors on canvas to paint a picture. True, he probably will follow a standard procedure in building mountains, shaping rocks and creating trees, but some of his own individuality will creep into his creativeness, even while he is copying someone else's method of doing things. The end result will be something individual and distinctive.

What goes to make up scenery? Both man-made and natural formations combine to form a realistic scene. Buildings and structures blend in with the earth, trees, and water to form the everyday world in which we live. This book is presented mainly as a guide to the modeling of natural scenery and will not dwell at length on man-made structures — yet they cannot be ignored: structures are one of the most important elements in realistic scenery. So, in planning your mountains, rivers, cuts, and fills, make allowances for realistic placement of structures.

Probably the simplest solution to the scenery problem, if the layout is small, is to cover areas on the flat part of the railroad table that are not occupied with track with green sawdust, or zip-textured grass, properly affixed to the surface. Then clutter up the whole scene with an array of buildings and structures such as might be found down near the railroad tracks. At least this may prove a momentary stopgap to the gnawing pains of hunger for a realistic model railroad. But once you have tasted even this elemental portion of railroadbuilding, you will find that it has served only as an appetizer for the more succulent dish that lies ahead — the completely detailed railroad scene shrunk to the proper scale for your locos and cars.

The dollar-conscious railroader will be as happy as a squirrel which has just discovered a new pecan grove to find that scenerymaking is probably the least expensive part of the hobby. His dollar goes much farther in the creation of scenery than in any other area of the hobby. For example: The railroader may shell out 50 bucks for a quality locomotive that occupies roughly a space 1½" wide, 2" high and 12" long on his railroad. Yet for con-

1-1 In the early days the imagination furnishes the background of mythical scenery.

DECATUR PUBLIC LIBRARY
JAN 15 1989
DECATUR, ILLINOIS

1-2 Later, the imaginative prop gives way; the railroader sees his layout as it is.

siderably less money than this he can completely scenic a room 14 feet wide by 46 feet long.

The reason for this economy is simple. Much of the material that goes into the making of even the best scenery can be salvaged from the scrap pile, and most of the tools needed are the most primitive sort which the railroader has already stored in his toolchest.

BEFORE any railroader starts his scenery, he should sit down and do a little serious thinking and planning about the kinds of scenes he wishes to create.

Is the railroad to be an old-time, or period, pike? Is it to be a logging railroad with its forests and lumber mills? Or should it be a mining operation with mines at one end, an ore processing plant somewhere along the line, and a steel mill at the other end? Should it depict the oil industry with its derricks at the wells, tank farms and refineries? Or should it combine several such features?

The size of the layout should determine this. Far too many railroaders, especially beginners, are carried away in a wave of enthusiasm and attempt to crowd too many features into too small a space. A friend of mine (John Page, onetime editor of MODEL RAILROADER magazine) once sent out a burlesque track plan poking a little fun at such haphazard scenery planning. John's comic layout included a rubber plantation, an oilfield complete with derricks, the Empire State Building, an airport complete with runways and ramps, a farm, Grand Central Station, the Rocky Mountains, desert wasteland, the Pentagon Building, the Appalachian Mountains, a waterfront dock, a general store, and the city of Los Angeles, all contained within an oval of track and sidings in a space 3½ feet wide by 5 feet long!

Even the rankest beginner with the imagination of a stale pancake can see immediately how ridiculous such a layout would be — even if it were possible to crowd all these things into a much larger space. Yet, strange as it may seem, I've seen some planning that was almost as farfetched.

Frank Ellison, one of the nation's topnotch model railroaders and a recognized authority on scenerybuilding and realistic operation, once wrote an article titled "The Fitness of Things." That four-word phrase seems to emphasize a warning that model railroad planners should heed. If you are striving for realism, do not attempt to crowd a conglomeration of unrelated scenes into too small a space. Make sure that all the scenes on the layout, considered together, form a realistic composition.

K. Phillips Kallman.

1-3 Most of the scenery on the famous O gauge railroad of the New York Society of Model Engineers was done by M. B. Wakefield. Road and fields are on a plaster foundation.

If you are modeling Death Valley and the Funeral Mountains at one end of your limited space, don't reach to the heights of the ridiculous by including a New York dock scene at the other end. "The fitness of things" also should be observed in detailing the layout after the model mountains, cuts, and fills are in place. If you are modeling a period pike, say the 1890's, don't include such details as modern autos, buildings, or structures in the scene.

On the other hand, if your railroad is a modern, dieselized version, it is still quite proper to place a few old-time buildings among the modern structures. Even an old Model T Ford is in keeping in the modern street scene. Explanation: The town skinflint refuses to tear down his old buildings and replace them, and he is

1-4 Bruzdenbleedn is the smaller of the two principal towns on my own HO railroad. The upper-level track and trestles do a great deal to provide variety in this scene.

Clint Grant.

hanging on to the first automobile he ever owned.

Ellison once said, "Scenery is a permanent thing and we ought to have a preview of what it is going to look like before we build it." If you are building your railroad to impress visitors and your fellow hobbyists with your craftsmanship, it is best that you model things with which you and they are familiar.

For instance, folks in the steel-producing section of the nation would not be nearly so impressed with a detailed model of a California oilfield as they would with a finely done scale model of a steel plant with its blast furnaces, rolling mills, etc. And, of course, the reverse holds true — folks in the petroleum states are always more impressed with a detailed oilfield with its derricks, refineries, storage tanks, etc., than with an excellently done model of the coal mining industry.

If you are *not* trying to impress visitors with your layout and are building for your own satisfaction, it still stands to reason that to build an accurate railroad scene, you should attempt to reproduce in miniature that with which you are most familiar — or else be prepared to do a whale of a lot of research on the subject if you desire an accurate model of the real thing.

In nature and in prototype railroading, the rocks, mountains, and rivers were there first, and the rails were the last thing to be added to the scene. The tracks were twisted and turned, made to rise and fall to follow the contours of the earth. In model railroading the reverse is normally the rule. Scenery usually is the *last* feature added to the layout. Therefore, it is a *must* in planning your trackwork that you should give some thought about the type of scenery through which your railroad will pass. We will go into more detail on this subject later in the book.

If you are striving for realistic scenery, the no. 1 rule to remember is to make your scenery look as if the rocks, hills, rivers, land, and ravines were there *before* the tracks were laid — not after.

Perhaps the most often asked question fired by the beginner at the experienced scenerybuilder is, "What's the best method of building mountains — painting — forming cuts and fills, etc.?" And the answer to that one is, "The method that enables you to get the most realistic results."

The old saying "One man's meat is

Clint G

1-5 Foliage and figures on the station platform lend an air of informality to a railroad scene. The enginehouse at Bruzdenbleedn was inspired by a John Allen design.

another's poison" most certainly applies to creating a realistic railroad scene. One fellow attempting to build his terrain out of cardboard strips covered with layers of brown wrapping paper and plaster — one of the classic methods — may fail dismally, but find later that he can get startling results by forming his hills out of screen wire or metal lathing covered with a layer of plaster. Those two traditional methods are now rivaled by a third, the hard-shell way of erecting terrain described in chapter 5.

The same thing holds true with painting. One fellow gets great results with water-base paint, but only makes a mess with oils. His neighbor, attempting to duplicate his friend's scenery, will foul things beyond all recognition if he attempts to use water-base colors, but he can produce a beautiful scene with oil paints and turpentine.

This also applies to the formation of trees and the creation of rivers, lakes, and streams. There are many methods of doing all these things, and the secret is to discover as early as possible the medium in which you work best — then stick to it and you'll find you will improve with each bit of work you produce. And if you don't know in advance the medium or method which best suits your talents, the only way you'll find out is to *experiment*.

If you can't make up your mind, get a scrap of plywood and build small hills by each of the three terrainbuilding methods. Which was easiest and which is the most realistic? Then experiment with different techniques for coloring your experimental mountains. After you've finished, survey the results and decide for yourself which method you prefer. Then follow that procedure in creating your scenery.

Incidentally, I think this idea of experimentation should be carried into

George Kawa

1-6 Bartlett Frost and the Detroit Historical Museum have done wonders with plaster on their HO railroad. Note the highway.

all phases of model railroading — whether it be building cars, locomotives, structures, or scenery. I know of several railroaders who have developed their own techniques of assembling locomotives and other rolling stock. They get far better results than if they follow the kit instructions to the letter.

Ellison once summed up the approach to scenery beautifully, pointing out that two of the most important functions of scenery are:

● Improvement of the realistic operation of the railroad by providing a background of structures that are used directly in the operation of the trains.

● Lengthening the route of the trains, making them seem to run through ever-changing countryside — giving them a feeling of going someplace instead of just chasing their cabooses or observation cars around an oval of track.

In addition to these two fundamentals, scenery can be made to serve the important function of turning what might be a scenic liability into an asset. It can be used to hide the truth by camouflaging unwanted pipes, chimneys, and beams which may rear their ugly heads in the center of the layout.

Chances are that anyone who ever builds a layout in either an attic or a basement will be confronted by the problem of pipes or columns rising through what otherwise might be a very scenic spot. Of course, the nicest solution would be to eliminate the pipes or columns — but in the case of supporting columns, the house might fall in on the railroad if they were eliminated. And as for such things as sewer pipes, well, if the model builder is *determined* to eliminate them, he might build a "Chic Sale" comfort station complete with half-moon decorated door out in back like Farmer Jones used to do. But even that idea

might not work well on cold nights. The next best thing to do is learn to live with those eye-distracting elements and disguise them as a part of the scenery.

Dick Houghton, a western pioneer in model railroading scenery, ran smack-dab into the problem of unwanted pipes in his basement layout. Dick solved the problem by building a scale-model circular stairway arrangement around the pipe and painting it silver. Then he arranged a cluster of adjoining factory buildings around the base and called the whole thing Thizz Pipe Works. The pipe itself resembled some sort of storage tank and looked very realistic.

One of the early O scale model railroad clubs in the East was confronted with the problem of a concrete column about 18" square in the center of the space where a town was to be located. The problem of hiding the column, which supported the floor above, was solved by fastening two wooden frames of 1 x 2's around it. Four sides of a building made of illustration board with windows cut out were tacked to this wooden framing. The result was a towering skyscraper which served as the centerpiece for the surrounding town.

On my own HO scale Texas & Rio Grande Western system in Dallas, I was confronted with the problem of two pipes rising through the floor and benchwork and passing into the slanting ceiling of my attic. One was a vent pipe from the bathroom below; the other, an asbestos chimney from the water heater. I carefully considered the aforementioned solutions to my problem but discarded both, since they didn't fit in with my scheme of things. The whole scenic scheme of my railroad was to duplicate as nearly as possible the rugged scenery found where the southwestern end of the Rocky Mountains trails down from Colorado,

through New Mexico, into the El Paso and Big Bend sections of far-west Texas. Either a 40-story skyscraper or a towering storage tank would be as out of keeping with the rest of my rugged, desolate mountain scenery as a purple-lipped bum at a high-society garden social.

These pipes were in a far corner of my attic, so I slew two dragons with one stone. I hid the corner and disguised the pipes by building Mount Grande — one great towering peak that reaches from the benchwork to the ceiling. Before and after photos show the result. Before starting construction of the mountain, I stood off at a distance and visualized just what it would take to hide the pipes and still appear realistic. I even made a few sketches.

In the photo, fig. 1-7, showing the pipes to be hidden, the white lines show roughly the contour of the proposed mountain which would be necessary to hide the distracting corner and utilities. Fig. 1-8 shows the result.

To me, one of the all-time mysteries of model railroading is why a hobbyist who will plunge fearlessly into the task of assembling a scale model of a prototype locomotive, where an error of even $\frac{1}{32}$" may spoil the realism of the finished product, is so completely discombombulated at the mere mention of doing scenery, where the margin of error can be an inch or more.

Let's say the modeler is building a locomotive in HO scale. If he is in error by a fraction of an inch in forming his smokestack, the whole thing becomes out of proportion and spoils the realistic appearance of his engine. Or if his piping sags or bends by as much as $\frac{1}{32}$", it looks sloppy.

But in modeling scenery (we're speaking now of earth formations —

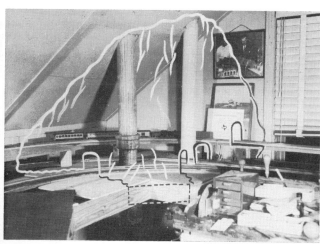

F. C. Peterson.

1-7 This corner of my own attic was a problem because of the position of vent pipes and the parallel curves in the trackwork.

Clint Grant.

1-8 I "imagineered" the future mountain, then saw the desirability of filling in a corner of the table edge before work was done.

not structures), you can put that scale rule back in the toolbox and play it entirely by eyeballing it. Let's say you're modeling a rock and you make it ⅛" or even ¼" larger than intended. Well, it still looks good—it's just a larger rock. Maybe you started out to form a rock roughly 6 feet square and you slap on a quarter of an inch more plaster than intended: the rock simply becomes an 8-foot rock instead of a 6-footer (in HO scale, that is). Actually, it often happens that the sloppier you are in slinging plaster and paint, the more realistic your scenery will appear.

"I'm no artist," a lot of guys will scream when someone suggests scenery. "I can't draw a straight line with a T-square and a ruler. Scenery ain't for me."

You don't have to be an artist to create scenery. True, it helps, and the trained professional artist can probably turn out a top product; but I've seen some wonderful results by fellows who have never made a sketch of any kind.

One thing you must realize is that in creating scenery you are working in *three dimensions*, which makes it easier. The artist in attempting to draw or paint a landscape must have a working knowledge of perspective and the other technicalities of his profession to be able to create on a flat piece of paper or canvas a scene that has form and body. In the same plane of that flat piece of paper he must make a gully in the foreground seem to have form and depth, and a mountain in the distance seem to recede. But the scenerybuilder is not working in a flat plane—he has the room to give his gullies and mountains actual form and body.

Besides, how do you know whether you're an artist or not? Have you ever tried? No doubt there are many musical geniuses wandering around today who have never played a note simply because they never tried. So don't succumb to that inborn fear that you have not the artistic talent to create real scenery. Don't be afraid if you can't draw a straight line— THERE ARE NO ABSOLUTELY STRAIGHT LINES IN NATURE.

Now for the tools that you may need. As I mentioned before, the most primitive sort will suffice. Roughly speaking, I'd say the following will do:
- Scissors.
- Putty or plaster spatula.
- Common table knife.
- Dimestore paintbrushes: ½", 1", 2".

If you elect to erect terrain by the wire screen method you will need

K. Phillips Kallman.

1-9 **Delaware Water Gap on the NYSME. Note treatment between track and water.**

a tack hammer (an ordinary hammer will do in a pinch). This and a stapling gun are needed for the cardboard strip method. When plaster is mixed you will need vessels for water and plaster. You'll also find uses for cleaned instant-coffee jars or something similar to contain colors, dyes, grass mixtures, and the like.

The scissors should be of the type to cut screen wire or cardboard, depending upon the material you finally decide to use as your supporting base for your plaster.

Actually, you can make the common table knife do the work of the spatula. However, the broader spreading area of the spatula will speed the work if the areas to be plastered are large. In

any event, the table knife is almost a must. Its flat surface is handy when it comes to spreading plaster in small, out-of-the-way places where a spatula may be too broad, and its thin cutting edge is the very thing for forming cracks in rocks.

You can use the same brushes for applying plaster and stippling it as you do for painting, providing you wash them out thoroughly each time after using them.

As you progress in scenerybuilding, you will find that you will improvise your own tools. Small bits of tin, pieces of wood, wire, and other objects all can be formed into modeling tools that will help you shape the wet plaster into realistic forms.

2 PLANNING AHEAD

THE most often neglected step in the creation of a realistic model railroad is careful advance planning of the overall layout in which allowances are made for the proper placement of scenery. The typical model railroader doesn't *start to think* about scenery until his trackwork is in, the wiring is completed, and everything is humming smoothly. But the empire builder who follows this course often winds up with some rather impossible scenic situations. He tries to make the scenery fit the railroad, and the result is unrealistic. Scenery so constructed usually looks just like what it is — something that was worked in as an afterthought.

Remember, one of the neat tricks of scenerybuilding is to *make it appear* that the scenery was there first — and that the railroad came later. Now, I'm not going off the deep end and suggest that we railroaders first build our plaster mountains and hills, and then blast tunnels with scale dynamite and build cuts and fills and lay our track last — but we should make it *appear* that was the way the layout was built.

By all means lay the track first, install wiring, signals and all other mechanical and electrical devices, and tune up the whole thing until it is purring like a high-precision sports car before scenery construction is started. But, before you drive a single spike or lay a rail, at least give some thought to scenery: where it should be; how much space should be allotted for it; and what type it should be. Such advance planning will save you countless hours of work and many a headache later on.

I've had many an old-timer in the hobby tell me that his biggest mistake was waiting until his trackwork was completed before he started to think about his scenery problems. One of the most startling examples of this lack of advance planning was an HO layout that otherwise was one of the most remarkable model railroads I've ever seen.

It was built by a fairly wealthy friend of mine in an attic room. He was an expert craftsman who knew how to use his complete collection of power tools. He was a perfectionist from the word "Go," and his benchwork resembled more a piece of fine furniture than a location for a model railroad. His trackwork was perfect

— he had switches custom-made by one of the nationally recognized builders in this field. The railroad was completely signaled with a three-color, two-way interlocked signal system. He hired an expert, professional electrician to assist him in its wiring. I do not recall ever having seen a derailment over his smooth trackwork in many, many hours of operation. And his track plan made possible very realistic operation and switching of trains.

Finally, the time came when he decided he should put in some scenery. He called in several friends whom he considered proficient in this field, admitting to them that the scenery problem had him stumped. The friends, experienced in the building of scenery, took a good, long look at the layout, shook their heads sadly, and admitted that they were as puzzled as the builder when it came to landscaping the railroad in a realistic manner.

Why? Because the builder had failed to give any advance thought to the scenery problem. If he had deliberately planned it that way, he couldn't have achieved some of the impossible scenic situations into which he had accidentally stumbled.

Most of his double-tracked main line was jammed too closely to the supports of the various upper levels of track all the way around the framework. Where tunnels might logically be, he had a maze of crossovers and switches. There was no room between tracks at his industrial sidings to accommodate the industrial buildings the sidings would serve — hence there was no apparent reason for the sidings' existence. Practically every upper-level crossing over a lower-level track was at such an angle as to make the construction of a realistic bridge impossible. And along one side of the layout, the highest level of track ran the entire length of the room along the very outside edge of the benchwork, completely hiding lower tracks on the back side of the layout.

This latter situation is illustrated in fig. 2-1. The best solution to this problem that the builder's friends could come up with was a series of bridges and rock piers, as shown in fig. 2-2; there was no space at the outer edge for simulating earth fills. This might have been monotonous—and monotony is one thing that must be avoided in scenerybuilding. In fact, that's what

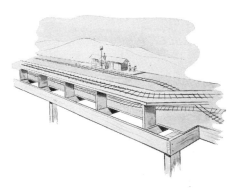

2-1 High track along table edge leaves no room for fills and hides yard tracks beyond.

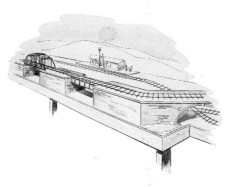

2-2 Same track can be treated as elevated line with bridges to provide visibility. Add roads or streams to justify bridges.

we're trying to do when we add scenery — avoid the monotony of plain tablelike trackwork.

EARLIER in this book, I advised that you, the railroad builder, give some thought about the type of railroad you want and the type of scenery you desire before you start planning the layout. Once you start your planning, concentrated thought should be given to the mechanics of scenerybuilding. Let's say you have decided upon the type of railroad it is to be, the type of equipment, and the general topography to be modeled — rivers, mountains, etc. In planning the mechanics of scenerybuilding, one must allow certain space for mountains and rivers, just as one sets aside certain space for tracks, yards, and engine service facilities.

One of the first and most important decisions that should be made by the modeler is what type of benchwork or table is to support the entire railroad. Is it to be a flattop surface, or is it to be of the open-top construction such as either the grid or the L-girder method?

The solid type of tablework has some advantanges in that it is easier to build. It requires only a simple, light frame under solid slabs of plywood. Also, the smooth, level surface of the table allows you to place your tracks where you please without regard to roadbed supporting risers. Disadvantages of the table are its lack of scenic flexibility, the fact that the solid top acts as a sounding board and makes the railroad noisy, and its construction, which can be both cumbersome and expensive in the long run, especially if used for a comparatively large layout.

While to a great extent the solid tabletop type of construction does limit scenery construction to track level or above, it *is* possible to include some below-track-level rivers, lakes or gulches by simply cutting out the desired places in the table surface with a keyhole saw. This method of construction is explained in detail in the book *The HO Railroad That Grows*.

Open framework is much more flexible and far better suited not only to scenerybuilding but also to supporting track at any desired levels. It is also less expensive and quicker to build. Most of the old-timers of model railroading prefer it.

The original open-top construction was the grid-frame system fairly well illustrated by fig. 4-1. A front and rear board run the long way along the framework edges and a number of joists span the gap between them. Three joists show in the opening at the left. Note that only the lowest surface, the river, is at the level of the joist tops. All track and scenery is supported on risers at various desired levels.

The L-girder method is almost the same in details of track support, but

2-3 "You have never reached the heights of frustration until you have attempted . . ."

the principal longitudinal framing members are made of two pieces each glued together like inverted L's. These are tucked under rather than butting against the joists — see fig. 5-12 — and a little way inward from the joist ends front and back. This simple change makes a great deal of difference in construction convenience because the joists can now be made any length. Thus the front and back edges of the tablework need no longer be straight. There are a number of other advantages, but full description is not proper here. I should add only that all screws go in from below; and since no pieces of wood are butted, there is no time wasted in fitting them. Any piece of wood can be removed if it is not wanted or if it should be shifted a little in position.

If the layout is to be large enough to warrant it, a combination of open and solid types of construction may be most satisfactory. Use solid tabletop for the areas where large yards and possibly the flat surface of a town or village are to be located. But use open framework where the rural or mountainous scenes with cuts, fills, rivers, and mountains are to be.

Another thing that should be con-

sidered is the height of the framework. It should not be so low as to make it awkward to climb under, for there's a lot of work that goes on *under* the layout — wiring, placing of switch machines. After the railroad is operating, there's always maintenance of these items.

On the other hand, the framework should not be so high that it is impossible to reach across it from the front. Even after the railroad is complete and scenery is in, you're going to have to be reaching over to rerail a car, clean track, adjust switches, and do the thousand and one other little maintenance chores that crop up on the best-operating of railroads.

This is a very important item to remember. It is almost a must to design your railroad so that every inch of trackwork can be reached, either from the normal viewing position or by means of access hatches in the framework. Special care should be given to the planning of access hatches back of mountains and tunnels. You have never reached the heights of frustration until you have attempted to get a train back on the tracks after it has derailed and tipped over on its side in a tunnel.

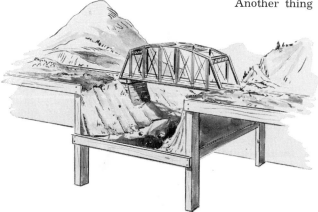

2-4 Lowered framework here and there allows for added interest of deep gorges, quarries, mines, and rivers below normal level.

2-5 On most layouts, scenery does not extend below the table level nor outside of the front edge of the table framework.

In my first layout I neglected to plan for such emergencies, and although it occupied a space only 8 feet long by 5 feet wide, I had to go outside the house and climb a stepladder to the window, then reach through the window and rerail my cars every time I had a derailment in my tunnel. This wasn't so good, especially on bitterly cold nights.

Most model railroaders prefer benchwork that is 40" from the floor or higher. Some build as low as 30"; others as high as 50". The benchwork height is largely an individual problem and in some cases may be determined by such things as a slanting ceiling in the attic. Ordinarily the outside frame of the benchwork is the same height all the way around the layout, with an occasional depressed section to accommodate a river or canyon as shown in fig. 2-4.

On most layouts, scenery does not extend below the outside frame of the benchwork or tabletop, as shown in fig. 2-5. The space underneath is hidden by curtains or shelving — or left open as a storage catchall. (This can be distracting to the eye if a lot of junk is allowed to collect underneath the layout and is not hidden by a curtain, paneling, or shelves.) However, in recent years some railroaders have achieved startling results by allowing the scenery to descend from the tracks and extend all the way to the floor, as shown in fig. 2-6. This type of scenery is especially effective if you happen to be modeling a railroad that operates in rugged mountainous country where the rails are laid along a narrow ledge high on the side of a sheer canyon wall.

And such real railroads exist. The most colorful example is Animas Gorge along the Denver & Rio Grande Western's famed narrow-gauge line between Durango and Silverton, Colorado. The fact that this stretch of rails was chosen by Hollywood for such railroad movie spectaculars as *Ticket to Tomahawk, Denver and Rio Grande, Night Passage* and parts of *Around the World in 80 Days* attests to its scenic grandeur. It is the ultimate in prototype for anyone wishing to model a railroad operating in one of the most rugged mountainous sections of North America.

In climbing from Durango's elevation of 6520 feet to Silverton's 9300 feet, the line twists and turns through Las Animas Canyon. At times the train is running along a narrow ledge of a sheer rock canyon wall that is but little wider than the width of the narrow-gauge cars. In fact, at some points the car steps swing out into space, and anyone standing on them can drop a rock straight down into the River of Lost Souls hundreds of feet below.

The trick of allowing your model scenery to drop off from track level to floor level would be perfectly fitting for modeling such a railroad as the narrow-gauge to Silverton — but it would not be in keeping with a railroad depicting flat country, such as the low rolling hills of some parts of Tennessee or the plains of Kansas, Oklahoma, or Texas.

If you do plan to extend the scenery all the way to the floor, it should be of the sturdiest construction; and it should have a narrow kickboard at least 3" high where it joins the floor. Also, this type of scenery should be used only at points on the layout where the operator is not going to have to lean very far over his trackwork for maintenance or rerailing cars. Otherwise he might lose his balance and fall through a mountainside.

In the advance planning of scenery there are few hard-and-fast rules which must be observed — but there are some good, recommended practices which, if observed, will eliminate a lot of knotty problems later on. A few of these practices are:

● Never place a mountain over a turnout or crossover — unless you have easy access to the switch from an opening in the rear of the mountain or a removable panel in the top. Switches and crossovers are a constant source of maintenance trouble on most railroads, and it is most disheartening to spend hours building a mountain only to find that you're going to have to rip it out the first time the crossover underneath it goes on the blink. Also,

1 x 4 KICKBOARD AT FLOOR LEVEL TO PREVENT ENTHUSIASTIC VISITORS FROM KICKING HOLES IN YOUR SHEER GRANITE CLIFFS

MCCLANAHAN

2-6 Scenery can drop from normal table level to floor level or any other low point for dramatic effect of mountain regions.

2-7 If you have to lean over too far to work, you might lose your balance and crash through the mountainside.

some sort of indicator is needed to show which way the hidden switch is thrown.

• It is a good general rule to place the highest tracks in the background and the lowest in the foreground nearest the spectator's edge of the benchwork. Reason: high tracks, when realistically treated with fills and mountains, hide anything behind them. Of course, in some cases it may be desirable to run a lower track back of a high one completely out of sight and use it as a "holding track" — that is, a stretch of track where a train can be run in and stopped for a given length of time to give the illusion it has traveled off far into the distance and disappeared.

• Make sure that *all* trackwork that is to be hidden or otherwise made inaccessible by the addition of scenery is electrically *perfect*. Rail joiners, which some railroaders depend on to carry the electrical current from one length of rail to the next, have a bad habit of becoming loose, oxidized, or dirty through the years, thus forming a poor electrical contact. It is most discouraging to have to demolish a mountainside to get at the seat of the trouble all because one little piece of metal ⅝" long has failed to do its job conducting the track circuit. A rule I have long observed is to solder flexible electrical jumper wires around each joiner that is in a section of track to be hidden by scenery.

• Allow for as much space as possible between low-level tracks that parallel high-level tracks. Tracks

LOWER TRACK TOO CLOSE TO VERTICAL SUPPORT OF UPPER-LEVEL TRACK.

BETTER ARRANGEMENT — THERE IS SPACE TO ALLOW FOR SLANTING FILL OR ROCKY HILL.

TOO MANY TRACKS TOO CLOSE AT DIFFERENT HEIGHTS.

2-8 Cross sections.

jammed close together, as in fig. 2-8, are difficult to scenic realistically. About the only solution is a perpendicular retaining wall — or a sheer rock wall. Either can be monotonous if the stretch of adjacent tracks is rather long.

• Test-run *all* rolling stock on your railroad through all scenic construction during the various stages of building to make sure there is ample clearance in tunnels and cuts, and along retaining walls. (This is *very important* and cannot be overemphasized.) Many, many times a modeler will set a tunnel portal in place on a curve and build a mountain completely around it, only to find that the first time he attempts to run his articulated or a long car through it there is not proper clearance to allow for the swing of the end. Or perhaps the big hook on his wrecker is too high to clear the tunnel. A common failure is to build cuts on a curve so narrow that they snag the ends of passenger cars swinging through them. So it's best to test all points where a problem of clearance might arise — from the very first time the basic plaster support of wire or papier-mâché is put in until the final coat of plaster is applied. (You'd be surprised how many times you'll find that an extra ⅛" of plaster has narrowed a cut or tunnel to the point where it is impossible to get certain rolling stock through it.)

• Allow yourself sufficient space for a bit of scenic treatment between tracks and the outer edge of the railroad table as well as between the tracks on the back side of the layout and the wall.

I've always considered 2" between the outside edge of the railroad table and the first track as a bare minimum. Not only does the 2" space allow for some sort of scenery, but it also provides a good safety zone, preventing derailed cars and locomotives from falling to the floor. Six to 8 inches would be a maximum, depending upon the scenery planned for the area. (These dimensions are for HO scale — increase or decrease them proportionately for larger or smaller gauges.)

For the space between the last visible track and the rear wall, I like a 3" minimum. This distance also should be determined by the type of scenery to be used. The higher the scenery, the greater amount of space there should be between track and wall.

Space for scenery should be allowed between tracks that parallel each other elsewhere on the layout. (I'm not referring to a regular double-track main line.) For tracks that run in the same direction on the layout there should be a space of at least 2" to 3" allowed between ends of ties if

they are on the same level. Tracks on different levels should usually be separated by a distance that is equal to at least the difference in elevation of the tracks. For instance, if a low-level track parallels a high-level track, and the high-level is 3½" above the low-level, then it is a good rule to allow 3½" space between the two tracks. This will allow a slope of no more than 45 degrees to any scenery that may be built between them.

A NYONE who has ever ridden the real railroads for any length of time and who has been halfway observant is aware of the gradual transition from town or city scenery to that in the country.

The train pulls out of the station, usually past a series of warehouses and industries, past freight yards and engine servicing facilities; then there are the inevitable rows of run-down shacks that seem to gravitate to railroad rights of way. Soon the buildings become more widely separated — we roll past a general store or two as we pass from the city to the rural areas surrounding it. And then we are in open country where the only signs of civilization found along the tracks are telephone poles, a few signboards, and other man-made structures such as bridges and culverts. The smaller the town, the quicker the transition.

Now, unless you have a model railroad room roughly the size of a football stadium, you can readily see that to model this entire transition in exact scale is practically impossible on the average layout. What we must do is condense this transition as compactly as possible in our limited areas.

When an artist sets out to paint a landscape, he often leaves out a tree or a brick wall or anything that might tend to spoil the composition of his picture. He may even add a tree or two to the scene if he thinks such addition will give better balance to his composition. Now, I've always contended that model railroaders are really artists at heart.

If creating a particular effect is the object, the artist has an edge over the photographer. The artist adds to or eliminates factors in his pictures, whereas the photographer's camera reproduces the scene only as it is. Admitting that we model railroaders are artists of a sort and it is well-nigh impossible to crowd *everything* into the three-dimensional pictures we are creating, then we must be rather choosy when it comes to the selection of what is to be included and what is to be left out of the scene.

What is the best method of advance planning of scenery? Very few people are so gifted that they can create their permanent scenery as they go along.

It takes a vivid imagination, plus a great deal of artistic ability, and lastly, a lot of know-how and experience, to plunge in and model a complete layout without at least a few small sketches or mockups to follow. I have known of a few railroaders who were able to do this, but they were professional artists or professional modelbuilders with years of experience behind them.

The average railroader finds it next to impossible to visualize in his mind just exactly how a three-dimensional scene will appear by merely studying a plan on a flat sheet of paper. Even the old pros at the game of building scenery often build a model or make a mockup of the scene.

Using a scale of 1″ or 2″ to the foot, it is possible to make a complete model of your model layout in plaster or clay and see in miniature just how your pike will look when it is complete. The main trouble with making a model of the model is that while it may show the positions and relative size of mountains, hills, valleys, cuts and fills, it doesn't give the builder too good a conception of the actual height of the contours on the full-size layout. For this reason the full-size mockup on the actual layout itself is probably the preferred method of advance scenery planning.

The best way to begin the mockup is to select a location on your layout where you have some particular scene in mind. Let's suppose it is to be a winding reverse curve which sweeps through a cut alongside one mountain, across a fill, and plunges into a tunnel in another mountain as in fig. 2-10. Using a fairly heavy grade of brown wrapping paper, thumbtack the paper to the layout framework around the base of the proposed mountains. Using boxes, wood supports, or even crumpled balls of paper, prop the mountain up to the desired height underneath.

Linn H. Westcott.

2-9 Few trees make "western" scenery. More trees make the same scene look "eastern." Note short tunnel at right. This breaks up the monotony of end-curve of the table railroad. Guest Terry Walsh examines basaltlike columnar rock mountain with builder C. B. Baird, Fort Worth, Texas.

Remember, this is all temporary construction just to give you an idea as to the size and shape you want your mountain to be, so anything goes at this stage of the game. You're merely experimenting. And don't be in too big a hurry — don't rush things.

In designing the mountain which is to have a tunnel, make it large enough to justify a tunnel — otherwise it will look as phony as a $7 bill. Real tunnels are bored only through mountains or hills that are too large to be passed through with an open cut. Too many model railroaders, in their anxiety to include a mountain on their pikes, build hills scarcely larger than the outside dimensions of their tunnel portals, as shown in fig. 2-11. The resulting mountain more closely resembles an inverted shoebox with holes at either end. Tunnels of this type look like those placed on a toy train layout under the Christmas tree.

2-10

2-11 Mountain not much larger than tunnel ends looks toylike.

The length of the tunnel is not as important as the height. C. B. Baird, the Texas bread tycoon who has built some of the most scenic layouts in the Southwest, had a tunnel on one of his layouts only 3 or 4 actual inches long (see fig. 2-9); yet it was very realistic because it was well planned. It bored through a rock precipice that towered hundreds of scale feet between gentler rocky slopes. Spectators got the impression that the builders of the railroad wound their tracks around the side of the mountain only to run smack-dab into a rock wall too high for an open cut.

After you have your paper mockup of the mountain area in place, stand off and study it for realism. If you want, let it stand several days and keep fiddling with it — pinching a contour here and there, crinkling it, forming ledges and crowns to represent the realistic rise and fall of the soil and rocks of the hillside and of ravines and gulches.

People in the eastern half of the United States are more accustomed to the gentler slopes of the Alleghenies, the Appalachians, the Great Smokies, the Ozarks and the Blue Ridge Mountains. These gentle, sloping mountainsides, with their occasional outcroppings of stone cliffs, are not nearly so rugged when compared to the more violent contours of the Rocky Mountains and the western ranges where sheer rock peaks and cliffs tower straight up hundreds, even thousands, of feet, looking for all the world like colossal stone skyscrapers erected by Mother Nature.

Naturally, when scaled down to model railroad size, the gentler, sloping hillsides take up more room on the layout than the more rugged mountainsides that shoot up into the sky at a sharper angle. That's one reason why so many modelers prefer the western mountain scenery to the more rolling hills of the East. You can produce more effect in less space.

Since space is at a premium on the model railroad, we should be very choosy in our selection of what to include in the scenery. There should be justification for every slope and ridge. Where you have mountains, you must have valleys — and where your tracks run from one mountainside across to tunnel through another, there must be some logical way of crossing that valley — trains don't run up one side of a mountain and down another like roller-coaster tracks. Engineers strive to keep all grades at a minimum in mountainous country. So in crossing from one mountainside to another one should strive to maintain as level a grade as possible.

This crossing from one mountain to another in model railroading is usu-

Clint Grant.

2-12 Terrain is often barren around a mine, as on the West Agony & Inchoate in Terry Walsh's garage in Dallas, Texas. In real mining regions this is partly because most nearby timber may have been used years ago for mine timbers, tipple framework, railroad trestles and ties, etc. But, in some regions, refinery or smelter gases may also kill vegetation. This isn't to say trees near mines are incorrect, for it's all a matter of circumstances. Note how a ridge of rock helps separate the main line from the mine spur and creates an illusion of greater distance between these scenes when viewed broadside. Anything that divides your space increases the apparent railroad size.

ally done over a fill or a long trestle or a bridge or some combination of these. In case you are not familiar with the term fill, the word is almost self-explanatory. It is merely a long level-topped pile of earth or loose stone that brings the ground up to track level. The word embankment is also used. The earth is usually taken from cuts and tunnels nearby, and the track level and route are adjusted so that as little dirt as possible has to be hauled from other places.

The angle of these fills varies according to the type of earth. Engineers, in constructing a real railroad fill, respect the angle of repose — that is, the slope that a pile of earth or rock

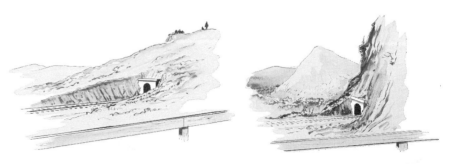

2-13 A cut at the approach to a tunnel should be made long if the hill has easy slopes too, but it can be short if the hill is steep as when made of hard rock formations.

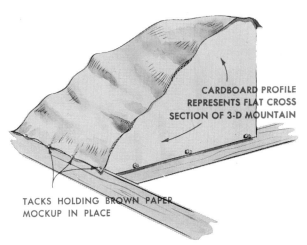

CARDBOARD PROFILE
REPRESENTS FLAT CROSS
SECTION OF 3-D MOUNTAIN

TACKS HOLDING BROWN PAPER
MOCKUP IN PLACE

2-14 Paper mockup for trial effect.

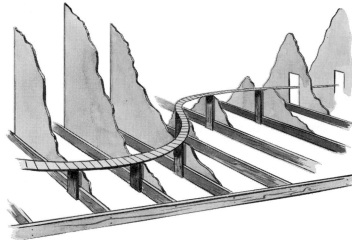

2-15 Cardboard profiles come next in planning.

assumes at its edges without sliding even when wet by heavy rains. In model railroading we can exercise a little artistic license and use a slope a little steeper than in real life. However, do not carry such distortion too far and model a nearly perpendicular slope to look as if it were constructed of sand or soft clay. If the builders of a real railroad piled the material too steeply in a fill across a ravine, the embankment would be practically leveled by the first gully-washing rain, leaving the rails and ties hanging in midair like a telephone line.

Perpendicular or nearly vertical walls supporting track should be modeled to represent either exposed bedrock or a man-made retaining wall. Loose rock or shale fills can have about a 45-degree angle to the sloping sides, while clay or earth fills should come nearer 30 degrees from the horizontal. Incidentally, earth fills are usually allowed to grow up in grass, weeds and shrubs, or are even seeded, to resist erosion.

Model your cuts, fills, valleys, riverbanks, and cliffs in mockup with brown paper the same as you did the mountains. Remember that there is usually a cut approaching a tunnel unless the tunnel is into the bare rock of a sheer, vertical precipice. The length of this cut will vary according to the slope of the mountainside as shown at the left in fig. 2-13.

Now the questions come: Should we build a mockup of the *entire* layout scenery before starting actual permanent construction? Or should we do it a section at a time, putting in the complete, permanent scenery at one place before starting on the mockup of the next section?

I believe this should depend entirely upon the overall size of the layout. In the case of layouts 5 x 8 feet or smaller, I believe it would be best to make a mockup of the entire pike first. But in the case of layouts of, say,

10 x 20 feet or larger, it would be best to work section by section.

By planning and completing the permanent scenery one section at a time on the larger layout, one is able to get a better idea of the type of scenery that should be used in the adjoining section to make the whole picture blend together nicely. It is sort of a case of one good idea leading to another.

It often has been said that the building of realistic scenery is not an overnight process. Careful study and thought as the mockup scenery is formed will result in the realization of its possibilities. Let's say that we have reached the point where we are satisfied with the mockup of the section or — in the case of the small layout — the mockup of the entire layout. The profiles of the ridges, hills, promontories and valleys seem to flow together as they do in nature. Now we must transpose this mockup into a permanent thing of plaster.

If you use the hard-shell method of erecting terrain, all you need do is erect wood supporting posts through this mockup to reach down to the supporting frame here and there, and then lay the plasterwork directly over your mockup. In an hour the plaster will be strong and hard, and the mockup can be removed from underneath.

It's not so simple if you want to erect screen wire or cardboard strips for a scenery foundation, but here's how it can be done:

Obviously the paper mockup must be ripped out before the permanent scenery is added. But the trouble is, the minute that mockup is torn away, the image we have created disappears from our minds. It is practically impossible to recall the size, shape, and relative locations of our hills, rocky ledges, cuts, and ravines.

We can maintain a rough record of the size and shape of the mockup by cutting a series of cardboard templates

or "profiles." These profiles, properly coded with corresponding marks on the benchwork joists, serve as patterns for the construction of the permanent scenery after the mockup is ripped out. They are actually cross sections of the scenery to be constructed — just as if you had sliced into the mountainside with a giant knife, as shown in fig. 2-14. They should be spaced together only closely enough as is needed to recall to mind the general shape of the hill.

As the paper mockup is torn away, these profiles can be fastened to the joists with tacks in the proper places where they represent cross sections. When the entire mockup has been ripped off and all cardboard profiles have been tacked in place, the result should look something like fig. 2-15.

Now if you intend to support your wire screening or other plaster supporting strips on supports sawed in a wavy line, these profiles can be removed one by one and used as a pattern for your jigsaw work, as in fig. 2-16. But if you intend to support your plaster mountain with light wood framing strips, the profiles can be left in place on the framework or table and used as a pattern guiding the erection of such strips. The screening is then shaped to the contours of the profiles as it is tacked to the straight framing strips, as is explained in fig. 2-17.

If the mountain is to be fairly large, it is a good idea to saw a wavy-lined

CORRUGATED CARDBOARD PROFILE SERVES AS PATTERN FOR JIGSAW CUTOUT OF PERMANENT WOOD SCENERY SUPPORT

WOOD OR
SCRAP WHITE PINE
FROM BOXES

2-16

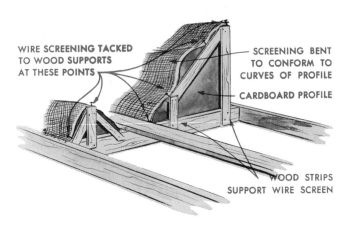

WIRE SCREENING TACKED TO WOOD SUPPORTS AT THESE POINTS

SCREENING BENT TO CONFORM TO CURVES OF PROFILE

CARDBOARD PROFILE

WOOD STRIPS SUPPORT WIRE SCREEN

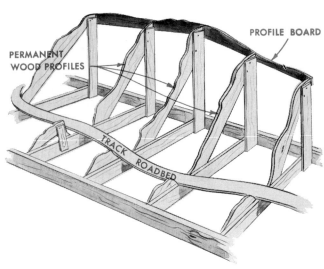

PERMANENT WOOD PROFILES

PROFILE BOARD

TRACK ROADBED

2-17 Wood framing is added alongside the cardboard profiles, which are a pattern for the placement. Some model railroaders have used cardboard only on small areas.

2-18 Another profile board reinforces the rear of the frames.

John Allen.

rear profile board and to mount it across the back as shown in fig. 2-18. With the supports in place you are ready to start covering the framework with screen or other plastering support. There are several methods in general practice and they will be discussed in a following section of this book.

Earlier in this section, I recommended that the construction of scenery not be started until all trackwork is in place and the layout is operating smoothly. As is the case in so many facets of model railroading, there are two schools of thought on this subject. Some old-timers in the hobby praise the building of scenery along with—or even ahead of—tracklaying, provided certain precautions are taken such as using Snap or Custom-Line switches or installing trackwork on removable roadbed framework. Also, there's the method of starting with a flat top, and then lifting the finished track to new levels. This is described in the book *The HO Railroad That Grows.*

I even know of one railroader who actually built his permanent mountain scenery before he laid a foot of track — somehow he wrestled ready-laid track into the proper curves and tacked it down in his tunnels. But he was an old-timer at the hobby and knew a lot of tricks of the trade.

Admittedly, building scenery as you go along creating the layout is a wonderful way to break the monotony of driving spikes and laying rail, something that can be a real chore unless you are a nut about trackwork.

One of the most beautifully scenicked model railroads in existence, John Allen's famed Gorre & Daphetid

2-19 Scenery preceded tracklaying on some branches of John Allen's well-known Gorre & Daphetid RR. Note dry washes.

line, was built scenery before track. But John is an old-timer at the game of building scenery and a nationally recognized expert on that phase of the hobby. He knew where he could build scenery in advance without encountering trouble later — and where track should be laid in advance.

The beginner who has never built a layout of any sort, who would like to follow this method of building scenery in advance of tracklaying should be warned of two very dangerous pitfalls that await the unwary who choose to take this route. They are:

● Clearances. If scenery is built first, it is more difficult to judge just how wide a space to leave for cuts, retaining walls and vertical rock ledges that adjoin the track.

● Obstructions to work space. Sometimes the beginner in his enthusiasm of creating scenery in advance of tracklaying may find that he has not allowed sufficient space in a newly built mountain range or cut for his hands to work at the job of spiking the rails in place. This is especially true if the builder is spiking down his track, rail by rail, on grooved Tru-Scale roadbed or on individually laid ties.

So, if you *must* build your scenery in advance, make sure there is room for your arms, hands, and tools to operate freely in any future installation work such as the laying of track, placement of switch machines, or wiring.

While the final plaster scenery is referred to as "permanent scenery," that doesn't mean it cannot be changed in the future. We have referred to the finished plasterwork as "permanent" so as to distinguish it from the mockup stage when we did our planning.

On my own railroad I have redone about 75 percent of the scenery — and before the final train makes its last run over my rails, I'll probably have rebuilt the entire scenery 100 percent. The reason for this is that the more scenery I've built, the more I've improved. When I look back on some of my early efforts I can see the mistakes I've made, so I want to improve on them.

Some of the rebuilding of my scenery has been minor — merely a new coat of texture paint over the old plaster, plus a recoloring job. Other changes have been major ones. For instance, I ripped out one stretch of scenery about 6 feet long by 2 feet wide that represented a rugged stretch of arroyos, promontories, and ravines. Where there was once only wild country there is now a sizable two-track industrial siding that serves a whiskey warehouse, a meat-packing plant, a small casting foundry, a sugar-beet loader, and an oil depot.

2-20 BEFORE: Early attempt at scenery was presentable. This makes a good way to rough out an overall scenic effect, leaving detailing to be done later.

Clint Grant.

2-21 AFTER: Later, I resurfaced the scenery and added rock texturing and trees plus a small freight shed and a pole line.

Linn Westcott, one of the real old-timers in the hobby, has long been a great advocate of rebuilding and changing scenery and track too. He feels it's a good way to keep on having construction fun without having such a big railroad you can hardly keep up with the maintenance. Incidentally, at the end of chapter 5 he claims that the problems of building scenery first, even before roadbed, are no longer so serious with new techniques of framework and scenery construction. The problems are all still there: just a bit simplified.

Well, then, just because you have built a permanent range of plaster mountains, don't be afraid to tear some of them out and add a lake or river in a valley if the urge strikes.

Linn H. Westcott.

3-1 One of the finest of layouts is Carl Appel's Norfolk & Ohio in American OO scale. The scenery holds together because all of it is based upon the kind of country the real N&W and C&O serve; in fact, many of the views are actual prototype scenes in miniature.

16

SHORT COURSE IN RAILROAD GEOLOGY

NO ONE would dream of attempting to build a model of a certain type of locomotive before first carefully studying the prototype to learn the location of the domes, piping, and the thousand and one other details that go together to make a realistic miniature. We must look at scenery in the same light. While it is true that there is more margin for variation in modeling scenery than in the precision job of creating a miniature locomotive, we should at least have a working knowledge of the earth and its formations before starting scenery construction.

If you are a creative genius with a good artistic sense and a working knowledge of the earth's formations, you can create your own landscapes out of your vivid imagination. But the average fellow, lacking these great gifts, should turn to nature and use some scene that actually exists as the pattern for his model. If you happen to live in a section of the country that you consider attractive and worth modeling, you are indeed fortunate. Weekend field trips with camera, sketch pad, and an attentive eye to detail will yield a wealth of information to be followed in creating your own miniature hills and valleys on your railroad.

But if the type of scenery you wish to model is not nearby, a fair working knowledge of your subject can be obtained from photographs. For instance, if you live in New England and your heart's desire is scenery of the type found in the Rocky Mountains of Colorado, and a trip west is out of the question, your best bet is a close study of photographs of your favorite scenes. Travel magazines such as *Holiday* and the *National Geographic* hold a wealth of information and contain beautiful color photographs and sometimes drawings of mountains. On the other hand, if you have a particular railroad scene in mind, Kalmbach's TRAINS magazine is a treasure chest of both scenery and prototype ideas that you can copy.

Travel folders issued by the various states also provide realistic drawings and photos of various mountain shapes. Some fellows may find it easier to work from a good colored drawing of a mountain than from a photograph. I often find this to be the case. In creating the drawing the artist has eliminated all but the most important lines to create the shape of the moun-

tains in the picture. Quite recently I needed a model for a backdrop painting of a rugged range of mountain peaks I was working on. I found my model in a Canadian National Railways advertisement in *Holiday*.

While such illustrations will give the modeler an idea as to the general shape and proportions of mountains, a study of the earth's geology is most helpful to those who wish to super-detail their scenery with unusual rock formations and outcroppings. For those who wish to go into this subject a bit more deeply, the National Model Railroad Association recommends two reference books: *Rocks, Rivers, and the Changing Earth* by Schneider, and *Fundamentals of Earth Science* by Thompson. You may find these in your local library. Another book, *The Earth's Crust* by L. Dudley Stamp, has many colored photos of plaster models of geologic features that give you a good idea of earth structure and coloring.

It's a good idea to observe the natural rules of geology when you build scenery, because this will insure a realistic effect. A visitor may know nothing about geology, yet sense something special in your scenery if it rings true. Perhaps the best reason for knowing a little about geology is to be able to make realistic transitions from one type of scenery to another. You can copy the scene in a photo, but how do you join it to the next scene? Another thing that justifies a little knowledge is that you find out things not to do. These are easily recognized if you know how the land got to be the way it is in the first place.

In the remainder of this chapter, Linn Westcott, who has made physical geography a sort of special interest,

will outline some of the things to think about as you plan your scenery. He starts with level country, then discusses more rugged areas and winds up with some comments on rock.

By Linn H. Westcott

In level country, the high places may be only 100 feet higher than low places miles away. Some flat country is almost perfectly flat, with less than a foot rise in a mile. Generally, the land slopes rise less than 5 feet in 1000, except on banks.

In this kind of country, any rock outcrops would be a freak. The soil may be many feet deep, with sand, clay, or gravel below, and more fertile soils on top where the weather, decayed roots, and erosion or cultivation have churned it. A typical soil color pattern is blackish soil at the top, red or yellowish clay from about 3 feet down to 10 feet or more, then dark, almost bluish clay below. In time the blue oxidizes to the same yellow or red as above, if it is exposed.

Rivers usually flow in broad, flat valleys, winding from side to side and changing course with every flood season. Often the curved bend of a river is left behind as an oxbow lake in the broad valley. Foliage may be lush and junglelike if there is much rainfall. Low areas are likely to be boggy. In dryer regions, grasses or sagebrush may be the predominant foliage of flat land, and low places may be mud or salt flats.

In such country the railroad can go in almost any direction, but routes with the fewest crossings of streams and swamps are preferred. See fig. 3-2. Railroads are likely to follow old trade routes from one river, mill, or crossroads town to another, and since no

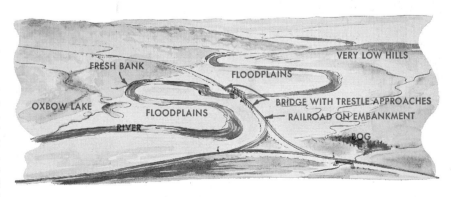

3-2 Watercourses are the principal obstacle when a railroad crosses low country.

Wallace W. Abb

3-3 Santa Fe's Chicagoan rides a low embankment to raise it above the terrain in low country near Lawrence, Kansas. Note standing water in drainage ditch along fence.

heavy cutting is involved to do it, a railroad will often turn as it approaches a river so it can cross via the shortest bridge practicable. It may turn the same way to align with the squares of an old town, but usually a model railroad is more interesting when it cuts diagonally through the street system. A "railroad town," being built with or after the railroad, usually parallels the tracks.

Important railroads are likely to be built a few feet above ground in flat country. This is both for drainage and due to the accumulation of years of adding ballast. See fig. 3-3.

The industries in flat country are mostly agricultural, but if the streams have some fall, there may be mills and factories that have grown on the sites of the original water mills, but which now use coal or electricity.

HILLS are mostly miniature mountains, or the fringes of mountains farther away, and so they possess

many of the qualities of mountains that we'll soon discuss. Most hills are places where bedrock formations have been cut away at the sides. Thus, rock outcroppings are likely to show above the streams, and they must show if any part of the hill is steeper than 20 to 30 degrees from the horizontal. This is because soils — including sand, clay, and gravel — cannot stand long at a steep angle. Usually the slope of a hill is steepest beside and above a stream, and it may round off gradually toward the top. Few hills are really dome-shaped, because smaller ravines, gullies, and draws cut the slopes on all sides. Hills are often formed in chains or complex masses just like miniature mountains, although not so steep.

A special type of hill containing no bedrock is found in the glacier-scraped areas from Minnesota to Massachusetts. These are piles of clay and gravel called moraines. Often they are long and narrow, all pointing in the

same direction. The Finger Lakes of New York run parallel because their basins were gouged by glaciers; nearby are long, narrow moraines pointing in the same direction. Sometimes moraines are perfect cones or long snakelike ridges. In all cases their slopes are gentle because they contain no bedrock.

Pockets in scenery take special at-

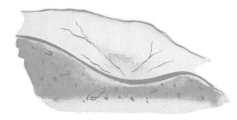

3-5 Pockets or kettles are rare in real life except in glacial gravel and lime cave areas.

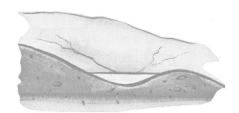

3-6 In less pervious earth a pond always forms in a pocket, then fills up as a swamp, then a meadow, and later may wash out.

tention. If you have a hollow in the terrain that could hold water — no outlet — it may need special treatment to look natural. Normally a pocket contains a pond or swamp, or a meadow where a swamp once was. Your only excuses for leaving a pocket hollow are if the land is a moraine, and thus is drained through the gravels, or is a sinkhole in limestone. Filling your pockets to represent pools, swamps, and flats adds considerable realism to the overall effect.

3-4 Hill anatomy. Notice how the cliff at left is caused by the same hard rock as bank at right of water. In this example, the rock strata are tilted, but could have been level.

WATERFALL OVER HARD ROCK
CASCADE
SOIL COVER
CLIFF
CLIFF
SOFT ROCK
FLOODPLAIN
SOIL
RIVER
CLIFF
HARD ROCK
SOFT ROCK
HARD ROCK
SOFT ROCK
HARD ROCK

All the debris that washes from the slopes of a hill settles in the stream valleys, and unless the stream flows steeply enough to carry the debris away, a flat-bottomed valley is formed. This floodplain is common along larger rivers and it is frequently the location chosen for towns and railroads. In crossing a country a railroad will often follow one flat-bottomed valley as far as it can, then climb a side valley to cross the ridge (by cut or tunnel) to reach another open valley where construction is again easy. Except for this, tunnels are rare in hilly country.

When a stream is too steep to form a flat-bottomed valley, it is very likely flowing in a course cut into the bedrock. It flows along the top of a hard rock layer, then cascades or falls past any soft rock to the next hard layer. This is because the soft rock is more easily washed away. There will often be outcroppings and other evidence of the same hard rock layers in the slopes nearby. See fig. 3-7.

In general, the streams in the broad valleys will drop only a few feet in a mile. Farther into the hills, streams will be narrower and steeper, while the rills down the hillsides will have the steepest bottoms of all.

Foliage will be most lush wherever water stands in pools and along the river edges. Trees will also grow greener in the hollows, where winds are low and moisture can be trapped. If there is a hard rock layer along a hillside, its pattern may show through the tree placement, since fewer trees will get a good foothold on hard rock than in deep soil.

In arid country, whatever growth there is will be along the watercourses, particularly just above any hard rock areas in stream beds. See fig. 3-8. In summer, water may not be flowing over a cataract, but some is likely to be trapped in the soil above the natural dam.

While railroads usually cross hills at a low level, going up one valley and down the next, there are regions where highlands make better routes. Parts of Virginia, Georgia, Iowa, and Missouri are examples. The ridges are very broad and long, and not too often cut by streams. Towns, roads, and railroads then prefer the high levels. Of course there can be no large gaps in the ridge, for a costly viaduct would spoil most of the advantage of the route.

Sometimes a railroad is located along a hillside, but this is usually only for a short distance, either to rise to another level or to follow a narrow valley when no better location is available. Such sidehill railroads are one long chain of cuts and fills, and perhaps a few trestles or even a tunnel

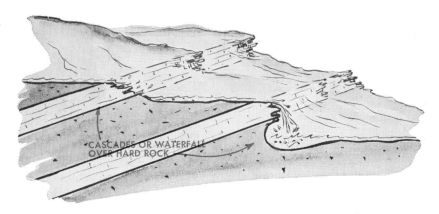

3-7 Streams fall over hard rock ledges.

3-8 Most water passes quickly in flash floods in dry country, but some flows under gravel at all times. Where stream bed crosses hard rock, moisture reaches the surface and a cluster of trees and other greenery appears. Pools may also form in these areas.

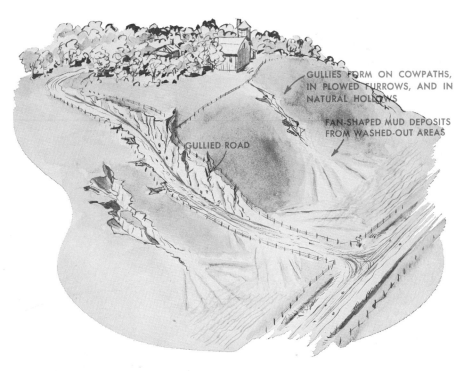

3-9 When grass on a slope is disturbed, it no longer holds soil, and gullies form.

are thrown in. In locating this type of railroad, the engineer tries to make the amount of earth needed for fills exactly equal to the amount of earth removed from cuts.

Mines, gravel pits, and quarries are common in hilly country. Agriculture and stock raising depend mostly on the slope of the land. An interesting scenic detail to add to your hill coun-

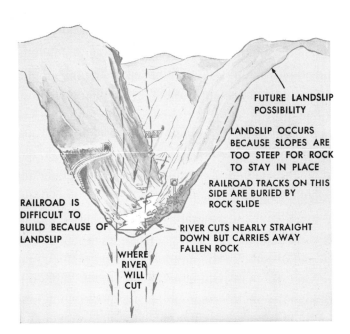

3-10 Anatomy of mountain V-canyon.

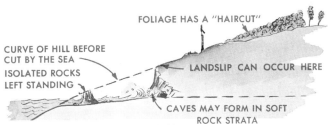

3-13 Idealized railroad route over mountain pass. Often railroads are relocated to reduce grades, as shown with dashes. In each case, a long, natural, easy-grade approach is used.

3-14 Anatomy of seacoast hillside.

try is an eroded field. This is where intensive agriculture has allowed step-sided gullies to form and cut away the soil from small or large areas, sometimes forming a veritable badlands. A similar erosion usually occurs where dirt roads go up a hill. For this reason, old unimproved roads may be as much as 10 feet below surface where they climb any hill. They have sunk from years of abrasion by hoofs, wheels, and the washing of the rains. See fig. 3-9.

IF you can imagine a block of flat land being raised 1000 feet or more, you can see just what makes mountains so different from the plains. With the ground lifted so high, the streams can do much more cutting as they drain the area. As a result, the streams cut V-shaped courses into the bedrock wherever they flow. Often mountains were formed by just such a process, so that their rivers actually record the meanderings of an ancient snakelike stream that flowed over the

original plain. As land rises, a stream cuts a path only as wide as itself; and it cuts approximately straight down. However, the sides of the canyon it forms are unstable, and over the years they fall into the stream, making a V-shaped valley (fig. 3-10). The slopes are usually only 30 to 45 degrees from the horizontal, though they look steeper. Only in rare instances is the rock so hard that nearly vertical walls remain: for instance, in the Royal Gorge in Colorado, where the steepest of the

3-11 D&RGW's Royal Gorge in Colorado.

3-12 The side of a mountain and the side of a V-canyon present the same problems to a railroad. In this Southern Pacific scene, concrete trestles cross landslide areas. Note how timber was removed around the track.

3-15 California hills slope into the Pacific Ocean along SP tracks near Summerland. Mud is hardening here but is not yet as hard as rock. Note line of land and treetops at distant point. Track nearby is on trestle.

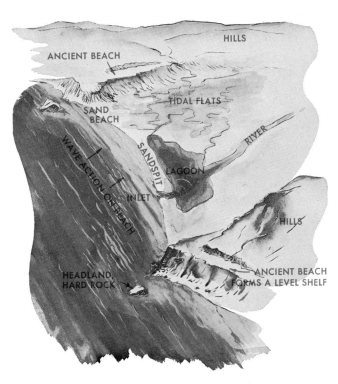

3-16 Anatomy of beach between headlands.

canyon walls repose at an angle of about 80 degrees from the horizontal (fig. 3-11).

When a railroad is routed through any V-shaped canyon, the locating engineer has a nearly impossible task: to cut a shelf for the railroad into the sides of a slope already so steep that it is gradually falling into the river. Retaining walls, rock fills, trestles (fig. 3-12), tunnels in rock, and even snow-shedlike gravel tunnels are used to tackle this problem.

Almost all of a mountain surface is rock with thin layers of gravel and soil on the ledges. This is where most of the foliage grows, but some finds natural footholds in the cracks in the rock itself. The stream valleys occasionally widen into a meadow, which is where most mountain towns are located.

Streams may be very steep in the mountains, falling hundreds or thousands of feet in a few miles. Since the maximum grade for a mountain railroad main line is only 100 feet in a mile and about 200 for steep branch lines, railroads often must double back several times in descending along a stream that falls at a more rapid rate. This accounts for loops, spiral tunnels, switchbacks, and horseshoe curves, as in fig. 3-13.

Ideally, a locating engineer building a railroad through the mountains will look for the lowest possible summit. Next he will look nearby for the broadest, easiest valleys that lead to the highest elevation that can be reached without expensive construction. Then he connects this high approach with the low summit by a track of maximum permitted steepness in order to keep the expensive part of the railroadwork as short as possible. Of course, the kind of rock that must be cut and the number of bridges and tunnels needed will also control the selected route, not to mention the availability of water if steam locomotives are used.

The most likely industries in the mountains are mines and hydroelectric plants. But the railroad may also serve interesting summer resorts, hot springs, and ski areas.

When you build mountainous scenery, don't forget to observe the patterns of the hard rock masses or layers, for they are very visible everywhere. They create waterfalls, cascades, narrows, ledges, precipices, ridges needing a tunnel; and they affect foliage in the same way as mentioned about hills.

GENERALLY speaking, the seacoast is just a level line drawn along the side of the hills or across a plain. The shape of the land below sea level is very likely a continuation of that above. If the sea washes against hillsides or mountainsides, it cuts away the material, forming a shelf just below water level with a cliff overhanging it (fig. 3-14). Salt spray stunts growth of everything for a mile or so inland, while strong winds give groves of bushes or trees a sort of haircut, very trim on top and sloping upward from the sea (fig. 3-15).

When the sea washes toward level land or river valleys, it forms a sand beach. Lateral wave motion tends to make the beach a gentle curve from one headland of hard rock to the next (fig. 3-16). It can even close the mouths of smaller streams to form lagoons and salt marshes. Larger areas back of the beach may be tidal flats that alternately flood and drain with

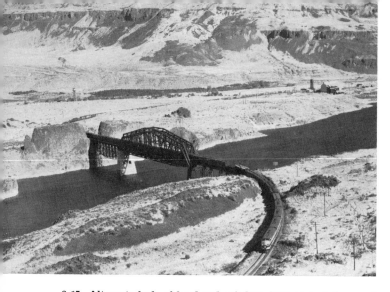

3-17 Alternate beds of hard and soft lava form rock shelves and walls along the Great Northern Railway where it crosses the Columbia River in Washington.

3-18 Sandstone and sometimes shale form pronounced horizontal layers in both natural and man-made rock cuts. Coal beds of the Chesapeake & Ohio lie nearby.

the tides through a maze of winding channels. If the land is sinking, the bays behind the beaches will be long tentacled affairs because their shore-lines are actually a contour line above sunken valleys.

In following a seacoast, the railroad must cross tidal flats on trestles or fills of riprap (loose stone filling). It must cross navigable rivers and inlets with drawbridges, and either tunnel through headlands or cut a sidehill route around them. Some coastlines have horizontal ledges far above sea level; these are ancient beaches now high and dry. They can be convenient places for roads and railroads.

THE rocks that cover the earth and expose themselves in the hills, mountains, and railroad cuts are mainly of two types. The original rocks were volcanic and are called "igneous." These include granite, ba-salt, and lavas of all sorts, including pumice. The color can vary from grays to browns, with some specimens of brighter colors. Often you can get the general effect of igneous rock by painting a base color, adding another color with short brush strokes in all directions, and spattering a third color with a toothbrush flicked with the fin-gers. If you do this, use a dull base color and slightly brighter spatter col-

ors. Three shades of gray are one pos-sible combination; mouse gray, dull orange and tuscan red are another. But the best idea is to examine the color of actual samples of granite or other rocks firsthand if you can.

Igneous rocks do not come in layers unless they happened to be formed on the earth's surface as lava beds. They usually break in all directions when blasted. Basalt, however, often occurs in cliffs or towers made up of hexago-nal columns familiar in Devil's Post-

3-19 Lava forced up an old volcano crater made hard Devil's Tower after softer rock washed away. Lava sheet formed in a long crack can produce a ridge called a dyke.

piles, the Giant's Causeway, etc. See fig. 3-19.

When rivers wash the debris from the mountains into the plains and on to the sea, another type of rock is formed. As clay lies for centuries in its bed, it gradually turns to rock and forms shale. Likewise, sand becomes sandstone, and gravel becomes con-glomerate. These rocks form in lay-

State Historical Society of Colorado.

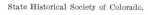

3-20 Note how Chepeta Waterfall has smoothed the strata of the rock below in this scene along the Black Canyon of the Gunnison in Colorado.

ers because the clay, sand, and gravel were originally deposited that way. Over the centuries most plains rise and fall, for the earth's surface is really on the move all the time. When a plain dips low enough, it is covered by the sea and then limestone layers or chalk are formed. These are the skeletons of minute sealife cemented into rock. Limestone occurs together with shale, sandstone, and conglomerate in layered beds.

The strata of these sedimentary rocks are originally nearly level, but due to the earth's motion may later be tilted or even folded into curves. In Pennsylvania the ridges of mountains are mostly the sides of these curves. See fig. 3-21.

Sedimentary rock makes colorful cliffs and cuts on a railroad because of the many layers in the pattern. The hard layers form ledges in natural cliffs and also cause waterfalls in stream beds. As in a hill, a hard layer forms a plane that can be traced all through a mountain wherever the plane cuts the surface.

Limestone is naturally a light gray color, but its surface may weather almost black due to decayed mosses. Iron salts may also color limestone a yellow or reddish tinge. Sandstone is frequently tinged with iron; clay almost always is. The colors "raw" umber, "raw" sienna, yellow ocher, etc., are actually clays ground into paint. "Burnt" colors are clays heated to drive out some of the oxygen.

Marble and slate are special types of rock. Originally they were limestone and shale, but great heat and pressure have hardened them into "metamorphic" rocks. They also occur in layers.

You might think solid rock is one big piece, but that's not quite true. Just as railroad rails expand and contract, so do rocks. For this reason, rocks have expansion cracks called joints. These usually run approximately straight and parallel in at least two different directions and from 10 to 100 feet apart. These joints are important when natural or man-made forces act on the rocks. All limestone caves, and many surface streams, choose their route along the joints, turning at the intersections to follow another joint. See fig. 3-23. Frost gets a foothold at the joints and enlarges them into more-visible cracks. Weeds and small trees force their roots into them.

The forces that cause earthquakes tend to tilt blocks of earth up on one side and down on the other. Sometimes there is a lateral shift. Naturally the place that gives is along one of these natural joints. This enlarges the joint and it becomes what is known as a "fault."

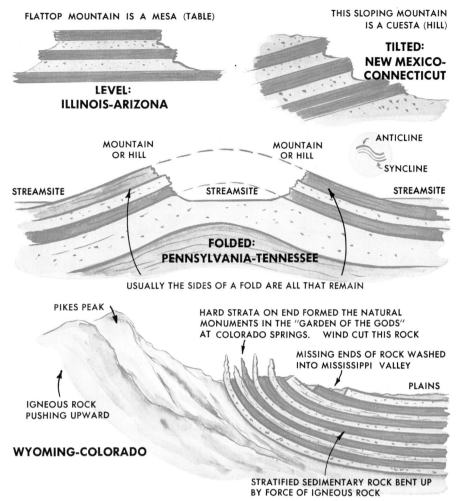

3-21 Strata may be level, tilted, or bent.

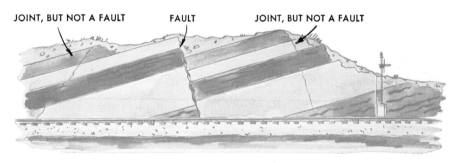

3-22 Railroad cut, showing joints and a fault. The strata beside the fault have the same sequence and thicknesses but with one side shifted upward. If the shift is slight, as here, matching patterns still show. Plants often grow in the joints and faults.

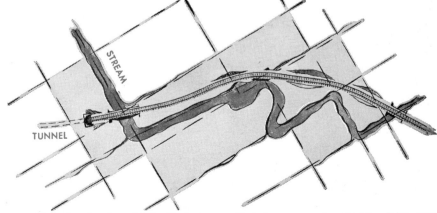

3-23 Map showing how joints (dashes) can affect the course of a stream. Joints may go at any angle, not necessarily at right angles nor as precisely as shown.

4 MATERIALS AND TECHNIQUES

THE final degree of realism in our scenery depends largely upon the manner in which we apply those all-important last coats of plaster and paint — regardless of how much advance planning we put into our efforts.

Realistic scenery is usually created in four all-important steps:

● Wood posts or a framework or skeleton of wood or metal is attached to the railroad table or benchwork, roughly outlining the contours we have decided upon in our advance planning.

● This framework is covered with either wire screen, paper, or cloth (usually burlap) tacked to the supporting skeleton. In the hard-shell method a layer of paper or cloth soaked in hard plaster replaces the supporting screen but serves the same purpose: to support finish coats of plaster applied next.

● Plaster or cement is spread over this covering and shaped into details, either by molding while the mixture is wet, or by carving after the plaster has set and hardened.

● The plaster earth and stones are stained; simulated grass (dyed and sifted sawdust) and trees are added.

Beginners in the art of scenery-building are prone to make three common mistakes which put them back of the old eight ball long before they ever start painting their efforts:

● They make their final coat of plaster too smooth and slick, or —

● They leave trowel or finger marks in the surface that bear no earthly resemblance to anything in nature, or —

● They allow the texture of the screen wire to show through the plaster. This results either from spreading the plaster too thinly over the wire or by not covering the screen everywhere.

During World War II, I had ambitions to be a camouflage officer, and I studied a few of the books and guides issued on that subject. I noted that the experts stressed the fact that texture in artificial scenery is as important as coloring. This is true regardless of whether you are building a full-scale clump of woods to hide a battery of artillery or whether you are trying to hide the benchwork on your model railroad with some realistic mountains and valleys.

All natural earth and rock formations in nature have texture. Only man-made creations, such as slabs of concrete and asphalt, are comparatively smooth. Texture casts shadows. From the tiniest blade of grass to the tallest pine tree, from the most minute grain of sand to the largest boulder — everything in nature casts a shadow: that is, it has a dark and a light side. If you need a practical example of this, lay a piece of smooth cardboard on your grassy yard. Look at it through a mailing tube to spotlight it. Then look at the grass adjoining it and note how the texture pops out.

Our problem is to scale down this texture to a high degree of realism. Texture can be overdone, of course. For instance, sawdust that is too coarse does not look like the smooth lawn it is supposed to be, even though it is dyed green and spread on your HO scale earth. It is too coarse — has too much texture. The bare earth itself has some texture, and this should be kept in mind when you apply plaster, lest you get it too slick and smooth.

Fig. 4-1 almost tells the complete story of the fundamentals of scenery-building at a glance. It shows in particular the method using wire screen over profile boards. Hard-shell work is a little different, but I'll leave further details of it to the next chapter. The methods outlined here are what might be called the "conventional" methods. Hard shell became popular relatively recently.

4-1 From left to right you can trace the steps in scenerybuilding. You begin with the framing, then add risers to support track and terrain at desired levels. Screen, burlap, or hard shell comes next, and finally come the finish coat of plaster and detailing.

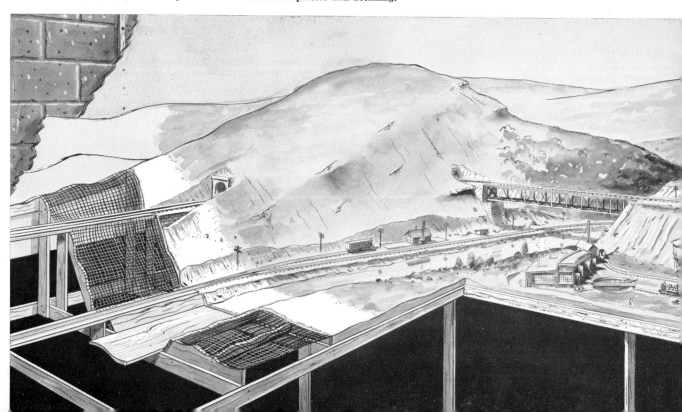

4-2 When profile boards are not used, most of terrain forming must be done by bending screen in midair, but crossbraces help.

It is not absolutely necessary to cut the profile boards in an irregular, wavy design, but doing so does make the final job of shaping the screen wire or paper covering a little easier. If you lack the tools to saw wavy profile boards, the supports can be straight boards as shown in fig. 4-2. However, if you use this method, bear in mind that the irregular tops of your mountains must be formed by bending the screen-wire or cardboard supports.

The method of building the supporting framework is more or less standard regardless of whether you intend to cover it with screen or paper strips. Some empire builders have used coathanger wire, looped and screwed to the framework, instead of wood; others probably have used such things as angle iron or strap iron. However, wood supports are by far the most popular and most adaptable to all types of layouts and scenery. For small areas where strength is not so important, you can use corrugated cardboard for profile boards. Strong supports are necessary if the mountain or area to be plastered is fairly large, simply because the screen wire (or paper strips) tends to sag when covered with a heavy coat of plaster.

For the covering material or "lath" over which plaster is spread, you have several choices:
- Screen wire as used on doors and windows.
- Hardware cloth, a heavier screen with ¼" mesh (for extra strength).
- Cardboard strips.
- Canvas or burlap.

Each of these methods has advantages and disadvantages. I personally use both the screen-wire and cardboard-strip methods on my layout. Where the scenery is likely to be bumped against by a careless spectator, or leaned upon, I use screen wire heavily coated with plaster for extra strength. But in those areas at the rear of the layout which will feel nothing heavier than the baleful gaze from the jaundiced eye of a hypercritical visiting model rail, I use the cardboard-strip method.

I have never experimented with canvas or burlap, but have seen some

very good scenery built from these materials. You must take care to disguise any curtain-drape effects of the cloth, however.

Of course, there are numerous variations of the fundamental methods mentioned. A variation of the paper and cardboard-strip method is the use of wide-meshed chicken wire covered with cloth or paper towels. After either cardboard or chicken wire is tacked to the wooden risers supporting it, the lattice is covered with several layers of brown paper or crepe-type paper towels soaked in a thin mixture of plaster. After this hardens into a shell, heavier plaster is smeared on and molded into shape. See fig. 4-3.

But before launching further into a description of construction methods, let's consider briefly the advantages and disadvantages of the plaster-support materials mentioned above.

Screen wire and hardware cloth

Either of these has the advantage of being the strongest type of construction. Supporting framework can be widely spaced and still support the wet plaster. The wire or hardware cloth is satisfactory for practically all covering materials, including cement or concrete.

This method has the disadvantage of being slightly more expensive than other methods. This is true if you have to purchase new screening from the hardware store or lumberyard. However, it is not more expensive if you have a supply of used screen which has been discarded by carpenters rescreening a home.

It also has the disadvantage of being harder to handle. Wire must be cut with tin snips or a pair of large scissors, and it is sometimes difficult to bend to the desired shape. By all means wear a pair of gloves (leatherpalmed work gloves are best) when handling the wire, for the rough edges can inflict very uncomfortable puncture wounds — and the rough surface of the screen itself can play hob with the cuticle of the nails when you bend

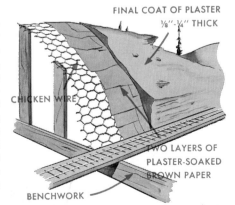

FINAL COAT OF PLASTER
⅛"-¼" THICK

CHICKEN WIRE

TWO LAYERS OF PLASTER-SOAKED BROWN PAPER

BENCHWORK

4-3 Plaster-soaked paper method.

the wire. When you use the ¼"-mesh hardware cloth, the plaster must have more body and the layers must be at least ⅜" thick.

Cardboard strips and paper

This method is probably the cheapest of the three. The cardboard strips can be cut from discarded posters or card advertisements which local stores throw away after they have been displayed for a short time. Brown paper torn from grocery sacks is an excellent covering over the cardboard strips.

The cardboard-strip method also has the advantage of being light in weight and easy to form in contours. Its chief disadvantage is its lack of strength.

Canvas or burlap

This method has the advantage of being comparatively cheap and fast. Also, if draped over a properly contoured riser, canvas forms steep mountain peaks almost naturally.

It has the disadvantage of needing many intermediate supports. Also, it needs sizing to give it rigidity before you apply the final coat of plaster.

Now, let's get down to actual construction methods. First, let's suppose you've decided to model a mountain and surrounding terrain using screen wire as a plaster support. I've found that before tacking the screen in place, it's a good trick to squeeze and bend the wire into irregular shapes. Ball it up and squeeze it (be sure you have gloves on); then straighten it out and bend again, and straighten out again. This keeps the screen from being too smooth and regular.

Next, tack the screen to the framework, using large flatheaded tacks. Some modelers use a stapler. Squeeze and pinch the wire to shape as you go along, driving a tack, squeezing the cover in shape to the desired contour, then tacking in place. Make sure everything is snug and secure, especially if you plan to plaster rather heavily.

With the covering support of screen wire in place, it's time to start slinging plaster. What sort of plaster should you use? Ask half a dozen old-timers in the game of scenerybuilding and you'll probably get half a dozen answers. The fellow over in Lousiana likes texture paint best. That Kentuckian swears by cement. The oldtimer up Milwaukee way is fond of molding plaster. A Kansas City fellow prefers wood-fiber plaster. And so your survey would go. Everyone seems to have his favorite, and here again it is a case of experimenting and using the type of plaster that you like best. In chapter 6 Westcott reports some recent findings about plasters.

Layout of Bob Barbour; photo by Linn H. Westcott.

4-4 Andy Uveges used a mixture of 20 parts asbestos powder, 2 parts plaster of paris, 1 part paperhanger's wheat paste, 9 parts water (all by volume) to make tacky plaster that he applied to screen with wet fingers. Lake occupies site of hump yard ripped out to make more room for scenery. Plastic water has not yet been poured into lake.

For many years the old standby was patching plaster mixed with asbestos. But in recent years there has been a big swing to texture paint. When I first started building scenery, I used gypsum plaster mixed half and half with asbestos plaster, but in recent years I've joined the swing to texture paint and use it just as it comes out of the bag.

Texture paint is rather difficult to carve after it has hardened. For areas where you intend to carve rock effects, stone retaining walls, or do any modeling *after* the plaster has set, it may be best to use patching plaster with no filler of any kind added.

Newcomers to the hobby, and those not familiar with the construction business, may be a bit confused by the name "texture paint." This term is something of a misnomer. Actually it is not a paint, but a plaster that comes in dry, powdered form and can be mixed to almost any consistency. It is marketed by many manufacturers, such as U. S. Gypsum Company and Wesco Calcimine Company, and comes under various trade names. U. S. Gypsum's product is called "Texstone." It is available at most paint stores and lumberyards, for it is used to give the

final finish to gypsum or sheet-rock wallboard in houses and buildings.

Texture paint takes about 2 days to harden, and it takes either oil or water-based paints beautifully after it has set. Some brands have absolutely no grain, while other brands may have a slight grit content. This varies with manufacturers.

As is the case with almost any type of plaster, texture paint loses its strength if exposed to air in powder form for any length of time. This is due to moisture in the air. If you buy it in small lots, a few pounds at a time, make sure your source of supply at the store is fresh. On the other hand, if you purchase a large 25-pound bag, keep it sealed and protected from humidity between plastering sessions.

JAB BRUSH INTO
WET PLASTER AND
WITHDRAW WITH
QUICK MOTIONS

SMOOTH PLASTER

4-5 Stippling plaster for rough texture.

4-6 Stippled rock is ready for carving.

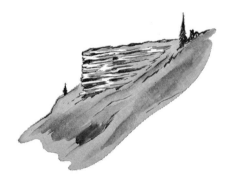

4-7 Final carved strata in rock outcrop.

And speaking of humidity, when there's a lot of dampness in the air, or if it is raining, that is *not* the time to apply glue-set types of plaster. Dampness in the air will slow down that kind of plaster's natural drying process and can cause it to sour and discolor. On the other hand, damp days are fine for true plasters, as they require moisture to do their setting. "Brief survey of scenery plasters" in chapter 6 shows which kinds are which.

Now let's assume you have decided upon the type of plaster you want to use and are ready to start spreading it on. How thick should it be? Here

again there are several schools of thought. Some prefer to mix the plaster to the consistency of brick mortar and apply it all in one coat varying in thickness from about ⅛" to ¼", depending upon the terrain. Others like to do the job in two or three coats.

I found that in working with screen wire I got the best results when I painted over the screen first with a fairly soupy, thin mixture of plaster about the consistency of cake batter, and let that harden over night. This fills the holes in the screen and gives me a good base on which to spread the thicker and heavier second coat of plaster.

The first coat isn't really necessary; I just like to do it that way. But if you're going to do the job all in one coat, *make sure your mixture isn't too thin.* If it is, it may flow right through the screen at low points and you'll waste a lot of material.

Any old pot, pan, or can of from 2- to 3-quart capacity makes an excellent mixing bowl for the particular type of plaster you've decided to work with. When I use a glue-set plaster such as texture paint I fill the pot halfway with plaster powder and stir cold water into it. As I add water the lumps smooth out.

Gypsum plasters, on the other hand, should be dumped or sifted into the water and not stirred until they have soaked throughout. In any case, the plaster should be thick enough that it won't drip through the screen wire; yet it should still be creamy-smooth enough to be spread evenly.

Arm yourself with the tools of the trade: a trowel or spatula (an old stainless-steel table knife makes a good spatula), an old paintbrush 1" or 2" wide, and an old tablespoon. Keep a glass or can of water handy to dip the spatula and paintbrush into occasionally to keep the plaster from sticking to them.

Dip up a liberal amount of the plaster with the spatula and spread it on. Working carefully, use the brush to spread the plaster and erase all trowel or spatula marks, for they have no place in the modeling of earth and rocks. On areas representing the rolling tops of hills, or places where grass might logically grow, the plaster should be worked out into a fairly smooth surface. But on the slopes where the earth is bare and is likely to be rough, stipple the plaster with the brush.

Do this stippling by dipping the brush into water, then pressing out excess moisture. The older the brush, the better it is for stippling. You don't want a brush that holds its shape. If the bristles resemble the hairdo of a Fiji Islander, so much the better. With little short jabs, punch and withdraw

the brush from the plaster surface as shown in fig. 4-5.

I stipple the plaster in practically all of my scenery, since I model fairly rugged country. Even the rocks are stippled. I first stick on a blob of plaster roughly in the shape of the rock. Then I stipple this blob of plaster as shown in fig. 4-6. After it has set a while and the plaster has become firm but not completely hardened, I come back and carve in the strata lines as shown in fig. 4-7.

Incidentally, plaster mixed for the formation of individual rocks and boulders should be of thicker consistency than that used to spread on the wire. It should be a fairly heavy mix, about like window-glass putty, so that it will hold its shape after the final molding. If it is too thin, the scribed strata marks will close up and disappear almost as soon as they are carved into the plaster.

There's another little trick that will add startling realism to your scenery. After all plaster is in place and all modeling and carving of rocks is done, *but while the plaster is still damp and has not set,* sprinkle the whole area with dry plaster powder. Use a flour sifter or strainer to do the job. Just reach into the plaster sack and grab up a handful of the dry plaster powder, put in into the screened sifter, and sprinkle it over the damp plaster. This gives an earthy texture to the whole scene and is especially effective after the landscape is stained or painted. This dry-dusting technique is the third of the four processes (thin plasterbrushing, dyeing, dusting, and erosion) which are elaborated upon in the "zip texturing" method: chapter 6.

WHEN it comes to modeling a rugged cliff or outcropping of limestone or sandstone in a hillside, even the beginner can learn more from a close study of both real and model scenery photographs than from thousands of words of written description.

Bear in mind the fact that the texture and carving of the plaster will be all-important when we get around to coloring the landscape. Thin oils in a turpentine wash, brushed on, will run freely into the tiny cracks and crevasses which form the texture of the final coat of plaster. The heavier color will sink down into these small fissures and crevasses, creating a darker color, while the raised portion of the texture will be slightly lighter, creating a very realistic effect.

When molding a boulder, rock strata, or a granite wall in a cliff, remember that the rocks and strata should appear to be a *part* of the hill or mountain and should be protruding from it, not sitting up on top of it, as shown in fig. 4-8. There are freaks of nature where a huge boulder rests on a tiny base apart from the surrounding terrain. Colorado's famed Balanced Rock in the Garden of the Gods near Manitou is an example. However, such freak formations are rare, and vacationers travel thousands of miles to see them. Usually huge boulders and rock walls have either a rubble of broken stone or an eroded earth bank around their bases, giving them a solid foundation.

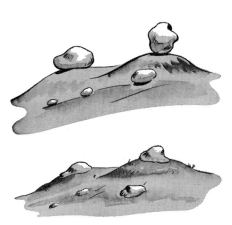

4-8 Be sure rocks are sunk into soft soil.

Those who can't visualize this sort of thing in miniature should try an experiment once recommended by Frank Ellison in one of his excellent MODEL RAILROADER articles. Go into the garden and pile a mound of loose earth about a foot high. Into this mound, press a few real stones ranging in size from that of a golf ball to that of a baseball. Cover these stones with more loose dirt. Next, stand off a few feet and spray the whole thing with a fine, gentle spray from the garden hose.

In just a few minutes this experiment will duplicate in miniature the action that has taken nature years to accomplish. The fine spray from the hose represents ages of rain. Note how the water collecting on the mound washes away the loose dirt. It forms tiny gullies down the side of the mound and the streams wash away the loose dirt, leaving the stones partially exposed with the earth hugging their sides and bases. Observe this action closely; then do your best to imitate it by careful plaster modeling.

Before we become too engrossed in detail, let's return to our discussion of the basic scenery description. We have talked about the screen-wire method of building mountains, valleys, and surrounding scenery. When I first started the scenery on my layout, which is comparatively large (14 x 46 feet), I used the screen-wire system. But in the finishing stages I turned to the cardboard-strip-with-paper-covering method. I can't say who invented or discovered this method, but I believe it was first publicized by John Allen in his article "Mount Alexander" [December 1949 MODEL RAILROADER].

The more I worked with this method, the better I liked it. In recent years I have come to prefer it. It is more versatile; and it is easier to model very rough terrain using this type of construction than it is using the screen-wire method. I disagree with those who say that the cardboard-strip method will not support heavy plaster. I have two large mountains on my layout, each large enough to conceal a card table; they tower from the benchwork, which is 34" high, to the ceiling. Both are made entirely from cardboard strips covered with paper; yet they support a very heavy coat of plaster.

The only weakness in this type of construction is that it will not stand pounding with a hammer by some visiting spectator's youngster. If you want to try it but are subject to invasions by that type of visitor, arm yourself with a stout Joe Jackson baseball bat and stand by to repel boarders.

The first step is to attach the wooden supports to the table or benchwork. Next, from heavy cardboard of the type used for window displays in drugstores and grocery stores, cut strips about 1" wide. Bend these strips to conform roughly to the contours you desire in your mountain. Tack these strips to the wooden supports and to the base of the benchwork or table.

Some builders prefer to use the strips tacked into place vertically only, as shown in fig. 4-9. However, for added strength, I place strips both vertically and horizontally, forming a sort of web or latticework as shown in fig. 4-10. That's where the hand stapler comes into use. Weave the strips in and out; where they cross, staple them together for added strength. As you build up the latticework, bend and twist the cardboard to form outcroppings of rocks.

With the latticework in place you are ready to apply the covering over which you will later spread the plaster. There are several ways of doing this. John originally tore pieces of old newspaper to about the size of his hand, soaked them in a solution of starch and water, and laid them on the cardboard framework about two layers thick. Similar results can be obtained by soaking the newspaper pieces in water only, then applying and fixing them into place by coating them and the cardboard strips with common flour-and-water wallpaper paste.

However, two major changes for the better have come about in this method in recent years, and Allen is following the new procedure in the construction of his latest Gorre & Daphetid RR. Several others, including Terry Walsh, onetime editor of the NMRA *Bulletin*, and myself, have followed John's lead

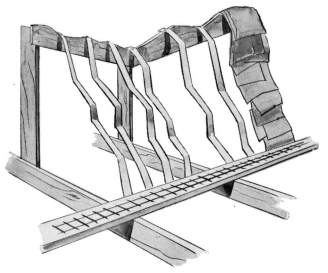

4-9 Cardboard strips used in place of screen wire — first stage.

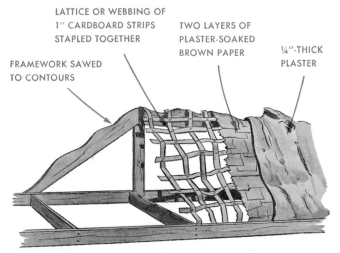

LATTICE OR WEBBING OF 1″ CARDBOARD STRIPS STAPLED TOGETHER

TWO LAYERS OF PLASTER-SOAKED BROWN PAPER

¼″-THICK PLASTER

FRAMEWORK SAWED TO CONTOURS

4-10 Cross strips add strength. Some use paper leaves soaked in glue as final terrain surface, omitting plaster.

in making these changes in procedure.

First, instead of using old newspapers, which are not strong to start with and which tend to become brittle with age, we are using common brown wrapping paper. Old brown-paper grocery sacks (if you have enough money left over from railroading to buy groceries) are an excellent source of supply. The brown paper is stronger and lasts longer. Crepe paper towels are also excellent, but not quite as tough as brown wrapping paper.

Second, instead of soaking the pieces of paper in starch or pasting them on with wallpaper paste, we soak the paper in a thin solution of plaster and lay the pieces over the latticework.

A good way to do this is to mix a solution of plaster about the consistency of thick waffle batter. Make the mixture in a shallow bread pan or tray. Tear the sheets of brown paper into irregular shapes about the size of your hand and immerse them in the plaster solution. At this stage of the game, it's a good idea to make sure the floor beneath the benchwork is covered with old newspapers, or some form of protection, to catch the plaster drippings as the pieces of soaked paper are applied to the supporting cardboard strips. Also, it's a good idea to cover any track which might be in the "drip area," either underneath the mountain or in cuts.

Lay the plaster-soaked pieces on the cardboard strips, pressing them firmly into place, pinching irregular shapes in them and doing some of the preliminary modeling as you go along. This pinching and modeling as you apply the coats of paper simplifies the detailed modeling that comes later.

Put at least two layers of the plaster-soaked paper over the cardboard strips. In places such as the bottoms of crevasses or gulches which will later contain a mass of jumbled, broken boulders, crumple smaller bits of plaster-soaked paper into balls and press them into place. After you have completely covered the supporting strips with paper, stop construction work on this particular area and let it harden *completely*. This may vary from 1 to 48 hours, depending upon the type of plaster used and the humidity in your area.

If the paper strips have been properly and thoroughly soaked in plaster, they'll dry rock-hard. The result will be a very sturdy shell over which you can apply the final coat, or coats, of plaster. I have found it easier to apply those last coats over this sort of scenery construction than over screen wire.

I usually apply one heavy coat of plaster ranging in thickness from ⅛″ to ¼″, spreading it on with an old 1″ dimestore paintbrush and stippling it

as I go. Before this coat dries, I go back over the whole area with heavier lumps of plaster, modeling in such details as stone retaining walls, heavy rock outcroppings of limestone and sandstone, and jumbles of lava flow.

The second coating of plaster should be mixed to a fairly heavy consistency, about that of ice cream which has just become soft but has not yet melted to the running stage. The plaster lumps for the detailed modeling of stone should be about as thick as window-pane putty.

Real stones and pebbles, pressed into the plaster while it is still damp and pliable, will add to the realism of the scene. However, be sure to use rocks or pebbles of a type and size compatible to the type of terrain you are modeling. For instance, a jumble of

4-11 Pressed cork insulation slabs can be broken off to make realistically textured granite rock.

small round pebbles piled at the base of a shale formation, where an assortment of flat broken shale pieces should be, would not be convincing. Stones get rounded from the action of rivers, ocean waves, glaciers, but not by rolling down a cliff.

Another trick that can be brought into play at this stage of construction is to crumble hunks from compressed cork insulation blocks and press them into the plaster.

Incidentally, slabs of cork, broken unevenly along the edges and laminated in layers, make an excellent representation of a granite cliff or rock face. I first saw this method used on the Detroit O scale club layout back about 1943. The members had latched onto some old cork life preservers, broken the cork into pieces, and built a very effective rock cut through which their trains wended their way realistically. See fig. 4-11.

Papier-mâché is another scenery technique. A mash of paper pulp is made and used somewhat like plaster over screen or other support. Papier-mâché is prepared by crumpling news-

papers and soaking them in water for at least 3 days until they are literally falling apart. The mess of paper pulp is then kneaded, like bread dough, with the hands until it is absolutely pulverized.

Handfuls of the mashed pulp are removed from the water and placed in a separate pail. Powdered glue and flour are mixed with this pulp until you have a mixture akin to biscuit dough. It is then smeared over the supports, screen wire or hardware cloth, shaped to suit, and allowed to dry.

While this is one of the cheapest methods of making scenery, it is the weakest, requires more and heavier supports, and is subject to cracking under accidental knocks and blows.

I should mention another method popular with some model railroaders and developed to a fine state by Borden Lilly of Toronto: "laminated paper." This is to dip paper towels in a glue mix and lay them onto the cardboard strips or any other support. Pieces of towel about 2″ x 3″ are torn off and dropped into a pan of water. Then they are dipped into thin wallpaper paste and applied to the scenic foundation a piece at a time all over the area until about six layers are built up. Rounded hill shapes are possible, and the final skin-like surface is tough and not easy to damage. It can be painted as is or can be covered with texture paint or plaster.

The last method of basic scenery construction that I will discuss is the canvas or burlap system. This method is also inexpensive, but it doesn't offer much strength. It needs more bracing and supports than either the cardboard or screen-wire system. The framework must be cut to the desired contours, as it is very frustrating to attempt to "bend" a piece of cloth and expect it to stay in place while the plaster is being applied.

The canvas or burlap should be tacked firmly to the supports; stretch it as tight as possible. I also suggest that the cloth be dipped into a paint, glue, or starch solution before it is tacked in place. As it is tacked in place one stuffs crumpled newspaper underneath to give it shape. After it has dried, heavier coats of plaster are applied, but very carefully.

There are two variations to this method. One is to use old rags dipped into some sort of stiffener and draped in layers over cardboard webbing or chicken wire which has been formed into the desired contours.

Another variation is to use plaster-impregnated gauze such as is used in making surgical plaster casts. This gauze is soaked in water and quickly draped over a cardboard strip or chicken-wire support.

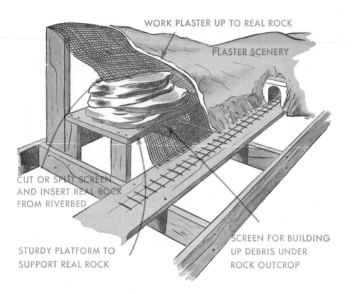

WORK PLASTER UP TO REAL ROCK

PLASTER SCENERY

CUT OR SPLIT SCREEN AND INSERT REAL ROCK FROM RIVERBED

STURDY PLATFORM TO SUPPORT REAL ROCK

SCREEN FOR BUILDING UP DEBRIS UNDER ROCK OUTCROP

4-12 Use care in fitting any real rock material.

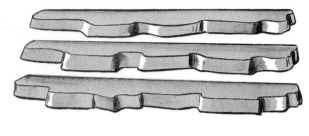

4-13 Celotex layers sawed out with jigsaw to make rock layers are improved if you brush their edges with plaster and carve more strata.

THERE are several neat little tricks that will add realism to your scenery, and they can be incorporated in any of the construction methods just described. One such stunt is the use of slabs of real rock imbedded in the plaster scenery. This is very effective if properly done, but the rock must be blended in with the artificial plaster scenery.

If there are any rocky areas near your home, look around for rock slabs that appear to be miniature replicas of the larger prototype. I know that there is a lot of red sandstone along the Oklahoma-Texas border near the Red River. It is easy to find chunks of the stuff — ranging in size from pieces not much larger than your hand on up to hunks that would require a truck to carry them — that are exact replicas of huge sandstone outcroppings that appear in this part of the country.

If real rock is used in the scenery, proper precautions should be taken to support it properly on a slab of wood, as shown in fig. 4-12. Place the rock in position *before* starting the plasterwork, and work the plaster up to the edges of the real rock to give the impression it is actually embedded in the soil.

Still another rockwork trick that's very effective is the use of laminated Celotex to simulate limestone or sandstone strata. Saw or break ½" or ¾" Celotex in wavy lines and build it in layers to the desired height, as shown in fig. 4-13. Brush a thin coating of plaster over the wavy edges of the Celotex, properly scribed, and sprinkle the whole thing with dry plaster while the thin coat of plaster is still wet.

Some modelers have made effective use of tree bark and partially rotted or decayed wood to get a rock effect. However, to make the most effective use of rocks or bark or any foreign material embedded in plaster, you must be careful to place the pieces realistically. Bark or rocks set too shallow and at varied angles do not appear very realistic, as shown in fig. 4-14. Rocks of the same type embedded in the soil usually follow the same general angle and slant as shown in fig. 4-15.

These artifices never look quite as realistic as real rock; and real rock is so heavy it is clumsy to use. Also, it is sometimes the wrong shape; yet you can't easily cut away a corner of it to make room for a new track or structure.

Fortunately for us, rubber molds have come into use. With these you can make castings of any sides of any real rocks — castings that are so perfect in detailing that with proper coloring you can't tell they're plaster at all. The work, except making the molds, goes quickly; and the castings have none of the defects of clumsiness, wrong texture, or great weight of these other methods.

This technique has two great advantages:

● It enables the beginner, or even the old-timer who just doesn't have the artistic ability to carve a realistic rock formation in plaster with a spatula, to equal or surpass the old pro when it comes to creating stone formations.

● It is much faster than carving. Even if one is blessed with the artistic skill of a Rodin, it sometimes takes hours to carve a realistic stretch of stratified rock. I personally have toiled one whole evening attempting to reproduce a rock wall area no larger than two pages of this book. Using the rock casting method, I have scenicked the same area in a matter of a few minutes, and produced more satisfying results.

Just who originated this technique is something of a mystery. I understand museum artists have been doing it for years to provide realistic natural scenes for their exhibits. I saw my first rock casting scenery on John Allen's layout years ago. Incidentally, most of those remarkable scenes of jagged canyons and rugged stone bluffs on John's fantastic layout were created with frequent use of castings.

Nature has a way of reproducing itself in miniature — a statement we'll repeat when we get to the section on trees and foliage. Some rocks have textures very much like much larger rock formations but in miniature. The casting technique provides an accurate and easy way to transfer these realistic surfaces and textures with all their intricate detail from nature to our artificially created railroad empires.

These rubber molds can be made in

4-14 Hah!

4-15 Oh!

the field if the desired formation is located in an immovable ledge.

Or, if formations can be found in stone small enough to be portable, the molds can be made in the privacy of your workshop where curious passers-by won't be wondering what the heck that nut is doing, painting all that sticky stuff over that old beat-up rock.

As you look for rocks to copy, you'll find that it is easy to train your eye to spot these miniature reproductions. Sometimes you'll find what appears to be a scaled-down face of a jagged granite cliff on the side of a lump of coal. (Lumps of coal are particularly excellent sources of stratified rock formations, and when cast in white plaster and properly painted and stained, they produce masterpieces of realistic rock reproduction.) Or it may be found in your garden. Or perhaps you'll spot an area no larger than the palm of your hand in a limestone or sandstone ledge somewhere in the countryside.

It isn't necessary to range far and wide on field trips to find these miniature rock outcroppings — though field trips can be fun. One of the best formations on Allen's layout was made from a casting of a rock in a ledge just across the street from his mountain home in Monterey, Calif. Roy Turner made some of his best castings from

4-16 Roy Turner peeled this mold from rocks across the street from his home.

4-17 This illustrates the "wet casting" method of applying stone castings to scenery. Before the plaster has set, while it is still damp and in the mold, it is pressed into place on the base scenery and held in place until the plaster has set completely.

4-18A After the plaster casting has set completely, the mold is very carefully stripped away.

4-19 (above) The dry method gives about the same result but may be easier to control for some modelers. Here the plaster is allowed to set hard in the mold first; then the mold is peeled away and the casting is applied to the terrain of the layout.

4-18B (left) The effect of a massive, jagged rock wall can be obtained by using the same mold several times in the same area. Monotony is avoided by turning the casting at slightly different angles with each application. All of the rockwork immediately adjoining each side of the retaining wall was made from one mold.

red sandstone found not 30 feet from his Oklahoma City workshop. Rock abounds almost everywhere, and it takes only a trained eye to pick out the possible model material.

I have several large red granite stones that I brought home from vacation trips to Colorado and the hill country of Texas for use as patterns for molds. On the other hand, many of the castings on my railroad were made from molds taken from limestone outcroppings only a short distance from my home in Dallas.

Once you have selected the rock you wish to duplicate, the procedure is simple. There are several brands of liquid latex on the market. Precision Scale Products, the firm that introduced code 83 rail, offers white latex. Another product is called Liquid Rubber: it is manufactured by Barstead Hobby Craft, Monmouth, Ill. Silicone rubbers can also be used.

Most such solutions are obtainable from well-stocked hobby stores. It is advisable *not* to buy more than you need at one time: a pint, a quart at most, will do fine; a little goes a long way. The liquid rubber tends to congeal prematurely if left in the jar more than a few months.

The only other equipment needed to make the molds are an inexpensive 1″ paintbrush, a stiff kitchen brush such as is used to clean vegetables (or a wire brush), and a jar to contain water.

First step is to clean the surface from which the mold is to be taken. Use the cleaning brush to whisk away loose dirt or grass that may be clinging to it.

Then wet the rock thoroughly. This serves several purposes: It completes the cleaning of the surface. It makes the eventual removal of the mold easier. It facilitates the flow of the liquid rubber into all those tiny cracks and crevasses that you want to reproduce.

While the rock is still wet, use the paintbrush to stroke on the first coat of latex. Make sure that the latex is worked down into all the fissures and cracks.

In all, about seven or eight coats of the latex are needed to make a sturdy mold. Each coat should be allowed to dry completely before applying the next one.

The time required to complete a mold will vary, depending upon the humidity and whether you are working in direct sunlight. If you are making molds on a field trip, be prepared to spend several hours in the open, as the latex dries rather slowly even under ideal conditions. In the field it is also a good idea to have several molds going at the same time. Once, on a field trip, Jack Leming and I kept about 8 or 10 molds building at the same time. By the time we had finished the base coat on the last mold, the first one was dry enough to come back to and apply the second coat, and so on. We kept busy going from one mold to the next, applying the next coat.

IF your layout is so large that some of the trackwork is out of arm's reach, then access hatches are a must. These access hatches are simply openings in the framework. They should be large enough that you can crawl under the benchwork and pop through them to

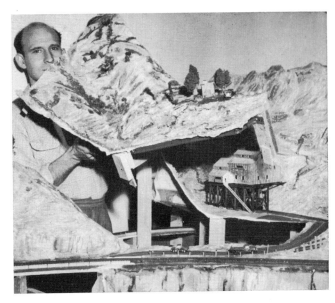

4-20 Liftout hatches with attractive scenery cover holes necessary for access. A highway camouflages the front end of Ken Smith's liftout on his pike in Cedar Rapids.

reach derailed trains, clean rail, adjust switches, or tend to any other maintenance that must be done. Usually 18″-square openings are about right.

Obviously an access hatch gaping in the midst of a completely detailed section of scenery spoils the realism of the show. The best way to camouflage these "maintenance hatches" is to cover them with liftout scenery. Liftout scenery is merely a scenic insert which fits snugly into the access hatch and blends perfectly with the surrounding terrain. It can be removed and replaced easily when necessary.

Liftouts may be of three different designs:

● They may be lifted and set on the floor or a table or hung on a hook overhead while work is being done in the access hatch.

● They may be built on a sliding panel.

● They may be fastened to the framework with hinges which allow the liftout section to be swung upward or downward out of the way. Usually it is preferable to swing liftouts downward, and the opening must be large enough to provide for this.

There's still another handy use for liftout scenery. Let's suppose there's a spot on your layout where there isn't room to swing a cat — not to mention a tack hammer or a paintbrush. It's much simpler to build a liftout section of scenery on your workbench where you have plenty of room to work, and after it is completed with coloring and shrubbery, place it in that awkward spot.

Changing the scene

Bob Hollin, a Dallas model railroader, makes still another use of liftout scenery. He has constructed several different types of trackside structures on bases of the same size. These bases fit perfectly into shallow

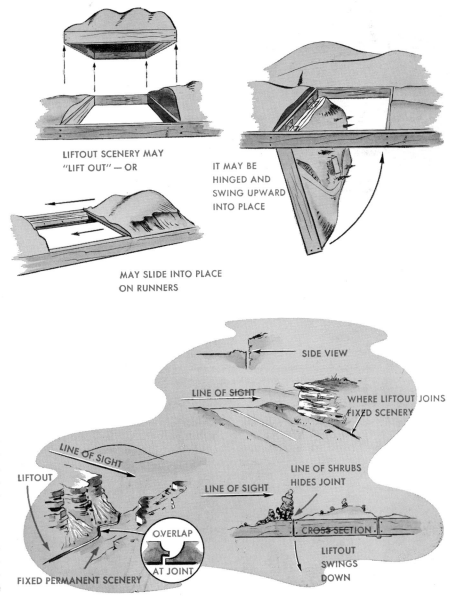

LIFTOUT SCENERY MAY "LIFT OUT" — OR

IT MAY BE HINGED AND SWING UPWARD INTO PLACE

MAY SLIDE INTO PLACE ON RUNNERS

SIDE VIEW

LINE OF SIGHT

WHERE LIFTOUT JOINS FIXED SCENERY

LINE OF SIGHT

LINE OF SHRUBS HIDES JOINT

LIFTOUT

LINE OF SIGHT

OVERLAP AT JOINT

CROSS SECTION

LIFTOUT SWINGS DOWN

FIXED PERMANENT SCENERY

4-21 Tricks and ideas for hatch covers or other liftout scenery.

4-22 **Rock on Bob Barbour's layout was carved while soft and sprayed from above with pale greens and browns for moss- and earth-color variations. The surface was then scraped with a spatula to reveal rock color in "weathered" areas.**

openings about a foot square in his plaster scenery. On one base he has a rock crushing plant; on another base, exactly the same size, he has built an oil refinery; on still others he has a lumberyard and a trucking depot.

On the night that Bob feels like running an oil operation, he sets the refinery in place on his layout and it blends in perfectly with the surrounding scenery. That night he runs tank cars from his oilfields to the plant. Next time he railroads, maybe he is in the mood to do a bit of lumber railroading.

He lifts out the oil refinery and sets the lumberyard in place and runs flatcars loaded with logs and planed lumber to and from the plant.

By a simple liftout operation that takes only a few seconds, Bob not only changes the appearance of his scenery, but also the type of operation on his railroad.

The secret of building effective liftout scenery is, first, to make it blend in perfectly with the surrounding terrain contourwise; second, to design the joints between the liftout and the permanent scenery so cleverly that

even the most eagle-eyed critic can't detect them. There are several ways of hiding these joining lines, as shown in fig. 4-21. Bits of lichen shrubbery glued to the top of the overlapping lines is a very effective means of disguising them.

In building the liftout section to hide an access hatch, it is best to complete the permanent plaster scenery on the surrounding terrain first. After the permanent plaster has set, build a sturdy framework of scrapwood exactly the size of the opening; make sure that it will slip in and out of the access easily. It may be necessary to nail strips on the permanent bench to serve as a support for the liftout.

Linn H. Westcott.

4-23 The Denver HO Model Railroad Club had this Rocky Mountain scene located only a few feet below the seats of Denver's Mayan Theater. Rock slides really look like loose debris here.

Baltimore & Ohio.
Clint Grant.

Linn H. Westcott.

4-24 The HO exhibit at the Baltimore & Ohio Museum in Baltimore is a model of Paw Paw Narrows on the Potomac. Scenery is most effective because it is a broad expanse of trees, river, and hillside. On most home railroads, scenery must be more compressed than this in order to provide for track and places for structures and industries.

4-25 Rock ledges at right in this scene at Cochran's Canyon on my Texas & Rio Grande Western are made of Celotex laminations, ⅝″ thick, tipped with plaster, scribed with lines, then painted. The use of the long, curved trestle helped solve problem of what to do where one track is high above another and they run parallel around an end-curve of the layout.

With the framework in place, form the plaster supports (either screen wire, burlap, or cardboard strips) so they will match the permanent plaster perfectly. The bending and shaping of the liftout may be done on the workbench, but when time comes to apply the plaster, it is a good idea to set it in place in the access hatch, if there's working room.

To prevent a plaster bond at the joints where the liftout meets the permanent plaster, slip a sheet of waterproof paper, such as cellophane or waxed paper, into the joint before applying the plaster to the liftout. After the plaster has been applied to the covering support of the liftout to the same thickness as that on the adjoining permanent scenery, allow it to dry. Then, and only then, remove the waxed paper from between the joints. Lift out the removable section and paint it. Hide the lines of the joint with shrubbery.

Large frameless liftouts can be made by the method mentioned for hiding a switch machine under fig. 6-13. If you do this, consider where you will place the removed cover so its edges will not get damaged.

IN building up the screen-wire or cardboard shapes of your permanent scenery, and later in applying the final coats of plaster, it is vitally important to keep in mind the contour of the land *before* the railroad tracks were laid in place. This is especially important in modeling cuts. It helps to give the impression that the land was there *first* and the railroad came *later*. This is illustrated in fig. 4-26. The dotted line indicates the slope of the hillside *before* the cut was made for the railroad.

If a cut is made through an earth or clay bank, the sides of the cut are more gentle than if the cut is made through solid rock or rock strata. A vertical cut through a clay or earth bank is most unrealistic in model scenery and absolutely impractical on a

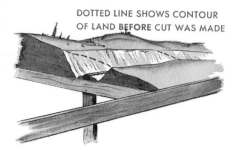

DOTTED LINE SHOWS CONTOUR OF LAND **BEFORE** CUT WAS MADE

4-26   SOME SORT OF DRAINAGE DITCH IS USED IN EVERY CUT

real railroad simply because the first heavy rain would wash the mud and clay down over the tracks. And, speaking of rains and washing, be sure to include drainage ditches on either side of the tracks through a cut. Cuts must be properly drained; otherwise the water flowing down the sides into the cut would soon back up and quickly form a lake completely covering the tracks. See fig. 4-27, right side.

In modeling an earth cut, scribe irregular, vertical erosion lines down the sloping sides, as shown in the scene built by Linn Wescott, in fig. 4-27. This represents erosion resulting from rain forming tiny rivulets at the top of the cut and washing small crevasses down its side to the drainage ditches at the bottom. Another method will be explained in chapter 6.

When modeling a cut through a combination of loose and rocky earth and rock strata, you can include a small landslide that has slipped down from the top of the cut and twisted its way to the bottom. This can be modeled by spooning some very thin plaster mix onto the top edge of the cut *after* the stone strata has been cut and modeled into the side. The thin plaster flows down the side of the cut and should be smoothed with a brush. While still damp, use the old flour sifter and sprinkle some dry plaster on the damp surface to give it texture.

Another type of cut commonly seen on practically all railroads is the cut and fill or "sidehill cut." This type of

construction results where the railroad is laid on the side of a hill which drops off rather sharply. The construction crew removes earth and material from the high side of the hill and uses it to fill in on the low side of the tracks as shown in fig. 4-28. The dotted line shows the original contour of the land before the tracks were put in place. Sometimes this fill is allowed to slant downward in the natural angle of repose of loose earth; sometimes, if the terrain drops off rather sharply, it is necessary to construct retaining walls of stone, timber, or concrete on the low side of the fill to keep the earth from washing away beneath the tracks.

These fills look more convincing if there is a wash area on the high side of the tracks. In many cases, retaining walls are built on both sides of the track: on the high side to prevent the earth and stones from washing down and covering the tracks, below the tracks to keep the fill from washing away. This is illustrated in fig. 4-29. Construction of these retaining walls will be described at greater length in chapter 9 of this book.

Coloring plaster

When the plaster on your scenery has dried or set completely, it's time to start coloring those hills, cuts, fills, and surrounding terrain. Some modelers prefer to include the coloring in the plaster itself. This is done by adding powdered "dry colors" while mixing the wet plaster. Advocates of this method point out that this colors the plaster all the way through. If it accidentally cracks, or is chipped, these mishaps don't show in the form of raw, white plaster.

That, of course, is a very strong argument in favor of the use of dry colors to tint the plaster. However, scenery "painted" in this manner alone assumes a monotony of color, for it is very difficult to reproduce the subtle changes in shades of the same color, plus the changes from one color to

4-27 Linn Westcott uses a soldering tool and a palette knife alternately to make rivulets in earth cut. Note drainage ditches at each side of track.

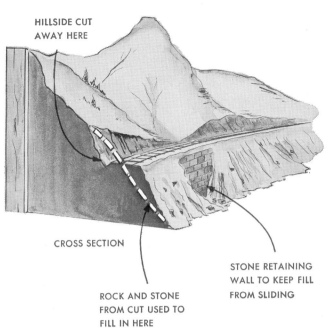

HILLSIDE CUT
AWAY HERE

CROSS SECTION

ROCK AND STONE
FROM CUT USED TO
FILL IN HERE

STONE RETAINING
WALL TO KEEP FILL
FROM SLIDING

4-28 Dashed line shows original contour of land which determines position of slope above and below railroad.

4-29 Retaining walls above and below track.

another, that we find in real land-scapes.

I suppose it would be possible to get those subtle changes using this method, but it would entail mixing a different batch of plaster for every color desired. The colors could then be blended as the various hued plasters were applied alternately to the screen-wire support.

For those who insist that their plaster be colored all the way through to guard against white cracks and chips, yet desire the subtle changes that only paint or stain on top of plaster can bring about, I suggest a combination of the two methods of coloring. Tint the plaster a basic earth color before it is applied by adding a good earth color, such as raw or burnt umber. Keep it on the light side, however. Then, after the tinted plaster has dried, paint or stain in the conventional manner which will be described in the following paragraphs.

Personally, I prefer to just go ahead and stain the raw white plaster and let the chips and cracks occur where they may. John Allen once told me that he thought these occasional white chips in scenery added to the overall effect. He likened them to the white, unpainted spots that appear in an artist's watercolor landscape done on rather rough paper—pointing out that they sometimes seemed to add snap to the composition and color.

Which is better for coloring the scenery, oil or water-base paints? That question is almost as old as model railroading itself. The answer, of course, is (as in so many other instances): use the medium with which

you can do the best job. Some can do a wonderful scene using water-base paints such as poster colors, or dry-powder paints mixed in water, or tempera or casein paints. Others, who can't handle the watercolors at all, can do a professional job with artist's oil colors in thin turpentine washes.

Each medium has its disadvantages and advantages, and here again, it pays to experiment. I started out painting my scenery with water-base paints, but later switched to oils. Frank Ellison liked oils. John Allen and Earl Cochran prefer water-base paints, and so on. Each modeler seems to have his favorite medium. If you do zip texturing you don't have to paint the plaster at all in the ordinary sense.

As far as expense goes, there is not enough difference between the cost of water-base paints and oils to amount to anything. A tube or jar of good water-base poster or casein paint costs about the same as a tube of fairly good oil color. It is the mixing agent that causes the cost of oil paints to be slightly higher. Water is the mixing and thinning agent for poster paints, and it is most certainly cheaper than turpentine, which is the best mixing agent for oils.

As long as we are discussing costs, let me stress that it is not necessary to purchase the most expensive imported tubes of oil paints to do the job. There are any number of economically priced "student oil paints" available at prices ranging from 25 cents to about 40 cents per tube which will do the job. And water-base poster paints cost on the average about 25 cents per jar. For-

tunately for us, most of the so-called earth colors are in the lower price range.

In my experiments with scenery painting, I've found that oils seem to produce richer and longer-lasting tones. Oils seem to blend more subtly than watercolors and produce a more realistic earth tone. However, some fellows may find oils more difficult to handle than watercolors. This is especially true of many newcomers to the hobby who've never done any painting of any kind.

The relatively new polymer colors are still only partly explored. They can be used like either oil or water-base paints, but tool cleaning and paint thinning is done with water. They dry waterproof.

The best way to find your medium is to experiment. Don't get the mistaken idea that it is necessary to take a full course at the Chicago Art Institute to learn how to paint a little bit of scenery. But a written description of how to paint scenery is something like trying to describe the color red to a person who has been blind since birth. It is very difficult to get across the idea of blending colors by the written word alone.

The trained artist has a head start on the beginner when it comes to painting scenery simply because he can look at a bank of earth and tell almost at a glance which pigments, when properly mixed, will imitate those colors seen in the ground. The model railroader who has never done any painting can do a lot of catching up in just one evening of experimenting before starting the actual painting.

ONE of the first rules that I always try to observe in painting is to do it under the type of lighting in which the scenery will be viewed. Certain colors lose their intensity when viewed under artificial light. This is particularly true of yellows and greens. Yellows that appear to be very strong when viewed under natural daylight seem to disappear almost completely when seen under an artificial light source from an ordinary filament-type light bulb. Also, some colors seem to change hues under fluorescent lights.

Now to get back to that one-night lesson in color perception. First, arm yourself with the tools of the trade. Old coffee cans or lids make economical mixing pans. However, if you don't mind spending a few cents, a dimestore tin muffin tray is a big help and serves as a palette for the paints. A couple of ½″ dimestore brushes, a can of turpentine, and tubes of raw and burnt umber, raw and burnt sienna, vandyke brown, yellow ocher, chrome yellow, and lampblack complete your equipment. Use the lampblack sparingly, as it is very intense.

Prior to the start of your experiments, slap some plaster on an old piece of screen wire and let it dry thoroughly. This is to be your "testing ground." In looking at the earth before, you've always observed that it is a sort of brownish color. Question is, what sort of brown? So, what you want to do in your evening of experimenting is to find out which of the aforementioned colors when mixed and blended with each other produce on the plaster testing ground a shade that resembles real earth.

The term "painting scenery" is actually a misnomer. What we really do is to "stain" scenery by applying a series of water-thin washes made up of oil paints and turpentine.

One of the big secrets of painting scenery is to apply the stains so thin

that they run together and blend themselves. Never make a stain so thick that it tends to be opaque when applied to the plaster. Several thin coats of stain over the same area are better than one coat that is too thick. You can always go back over an area that is too light and darken it up with additional coats. But if you get it too dark with the first coat, it takes an expert to lighten it. Usually the simplest way to lighten an area is to brush on another thin coat of plaster, let it dry, and start all over again.

Squeeze out only about an inch of paint from each tube into the tins — keeping the colors separate, of course. Into each pan, pour one third of a cupful of turpentine and mix thoroughly with the paint you've squeezed from the tube, making a thin wash. Keep a separate tray of clear turpentine handy to wash out the brush after each color has been applied.

First, experiment with the umbers — raw and burnt. These are a "blacker brown." Also, include in this group a vandyke brown wash. Dip into the raw umber wash and draw the brush across the white plaster. Right next to it, repeat with a dip of the burnt umber. Now try the vandyke brown. Notice the difference in the colors. Repeat the experiment with test smears so close together that the edges run together. Note how they blend. See fig. 4-30.

Next, run the same test with the siennas — raw and burnt. These are also brown, but have a more definite reddish cast. Now try short alternate streaks of all five colors on the plaster, applied so closely together that they run together as they are washed on. Streak on an umber, then a sienna, and note how they blend.

Repeat the experiment using the chrome yellows and yellow ochers to lighten the siennas and umbers. It might be a good idea to go out into the

yard and scoop up a handful of real dirt from the garden, bring it in and see what combinations of colors are needed to match it.

In some parts of the country it may be necessary to mix in a little indian red to match the color of the soil. This is particularly true in many parts of the West and in the deep South where some soils are almost a brilliant red.

Once you learn the knack of applying the stains and getting the different color effects that use of the siennas and umbers produce, you're about ready to start your scenery painting. Those who are not trained artists may find it a bit difficult to recall just what color is needed for certain effects. So, as a handy reference, here's a chart:

Soil colors

Browns:	Raw umber, burnt umber and vandyke brown.
Rich brown:	Burnt umber mixed with burnt sienna.
Reddish brown:	Burnt and raw siennas.
Reds:	Indian red, scarlet. (Various shades can be obtained by mixing in orange and a bit of burnt sienna.)
Black:	Vandyke brown, lampblack.
Tan:	Heavy raw umber stain.
Gray:	Thin raw umber stain; also thin wash of lampblack.

Rock and stone strata colors

Gray limestone:	Stain with very, very thin wash of lampblack first; then tint with extra-thin washes of ultramarine blue and burnt sienna.
Red sandstone:	Indian red with burnt sienna; sometimes burnt sienna alone will do the job.
Brown sandstone:	Vandyke brown wash with small amount of orange added.

BS — BURNT SIENNA
BU — BURNT UMBER
VB — VANDYKE BROWN
YO — YELLOW OCHER
BK — LAMPBLACK — VERY THIN
RS — RAW SIENNA
RU — RAW UMBER

4-30 **Typical arrangement of dabs of color. Let them blend together while wet for most natural effect of rock variations.**

Art Schmidt.

4-31 **Gordon Odegard used side of putty knife to carve shale or slatelike strata in this bayside rockwork. Most workers do carving while plaster is still soft, make final touches when hard.**

Linn H. Westcott.

4-32 **Igneous rock carved by Billi Bowen at the Bay Ridge club in Brooklyn.**

Yellow sandstone:	Light chrome yellow with vandyke brown.
Gray granite:	Thin wash of lamp-black first, followed with tint of pale ultramarine blue.
Blue granite:	Ultramarine blue and lampblack mixed to obtain a medium-heavy stain.
Red granite:	Claret applied very strong.
Shale:	Burnt sienna blended with vandyke brown.
Basalt:	Dark gray stain made with payne's gray streaked with heavy blue-black.

One thing to keep in mind while painting scenery is to avoid monotony in color. That's one of the big reasons stippled plaster representing a rocky surface is so much more realistic than a perfectly smooth surface. Stippling is nothing more than thousands of tiny little mounds. The thin color washes flow over them in uneven tones, leaving a light hue at the peaks and puddling up to create a darker shade in the crevasses.

In applying my stains, I do as little spreading of the paint with the brushes as possible. Instead, I jab brushfuls

of different tints at random spots and allow the thin washes to flow together, blending themselves. Fig. 4-30 illustrates this technique. Of course, it is necessary to do *some* brushing, particularly in spots where the natural flow of the stain fails to come together. But for the most part it is best to just press the brush loaded with stain against the raw, white plaster.

Don't be alarmed if your scenery looks slick and a bit wet immediately after the oil stains are applied. This type of stain dries rapidly, and soon takes on a perfectly flat, earthy appearance.

IN painting scenery with water-base paints, a slightly different technique is used. Basically we use the same hues. However, the shading and blending must be done with the brush, rather than allowing the washes to flow together, blending themselves.

Water-base paints are applied thicker. Apply the base color, say burnt umber; then dip the brush in white paint and smear over the rock formations, lightening the high spots. Other hues can be worked in the same manner.

Here again, the scenerybuilder can learn more from experimenting on a piece of scrap plaster than from reading hundreds of words of description of the technique of water-base painting. Water-base painting probably demands more skill with the brush than tinting with transparent oil stains. (Never attempt to use glossy household paints or varnishes to paint scenery.)

One of the most realistic little scenes, and a great favorite with most modelers, is an outcropping of gray limestone set in a bank of reddish earth. Stain the limestone first. Apply a very, very thin coat of lampblack stain. This will turn the high, flat surfaces of the limestone a realistic gray, and the wash will gather in heavier shades in the horizontal strata cracks, forming realistic shadows. Another thin wash of burnt sienna can be added — and if a bluer tinge is desired, a very thin wash of ultramarine blue can be added. Be careful with that blue; blue is a very intense color, and a little goes a long way. This is more especially true of prussian blue than of any other color.

Let's refer to fig. 4-34 for the completion of this little scene. After the limestone has been properly stained, use a fairly heavy stain of *raw* umber — that doesn't run too much — on the top of the rock; you might even brush on some color straight from the tube. This represents a layer of deep, almost black-brown earthen soil that is on top of the rock. This will later be covered with grass. This is designated as area A in the illustration.

Now, starting at the base of the rock, designated as area B, apply alternate washes of the two umbers, vandyke brown, and liberal amounts of burnt sienna. The final result is a realistic conglomeration of colors such as is commonly seen in many parts of the West.

Another little stunt that I've used to give snap to my oil-stained scenery is to dry-brush certain areas with white poster paint *after* the oil stain has dried completely. Using a completely dry brush, I dip it into the jar of water-base white poster paint. Then, on a flat surface such as a piece of scrap cardboard, I work the brush back and forth until the bristles are

fairly well filled with the poster paint. Finally, when the white paint is almost completely dry, I swipe the brush across the face of the stone. This must be done ever so lightly, just barely allowing the bristles to touch the high points of the painted plaster. The effect is white highlights on the face of the stone.

This "dry brush" technique is an art in itself, and one who has never attempted it should spend some time practicing on a piece of scrap scenery before trying it.

I also use this dry-brush technique over some earthen areas. I mix a bit of yellow ocher or burnt umber with the white, then ever so lightly dry-brush the earthen area. The result gives the effect of tiny veins of clay intertwined with the basic earth color. Also, this same technique can give the impression of thousands of tiny bits of shale or limestone which have broken off and become embedded in the darker earth.

The whole trick in this dry-brushing

technique is to hit the high spots in the rough plaster without getting the lighter paint down into the crevasses. This is illustrated in fig. 4-35.

All sections of your plaster scenery should be stained, regardless of whether or not they will be covered later with grass.

Most of us who live in large cities are too inclined to think of grass in terms of well-kept, billiard-tabletop-smooth green expanses that more resemble a first-class golf course putting green. But remember, we are modeling the grass that grows wild in the open country. Such grass grows in irregular splotches, and its green expanse is often broken by areas of the rich brown earth showing through. The grass itself varies in color in the same area, ranging from a pale yellow to a deep olive green.

Dyed sawdust has been an old standby in model railroading for years when it comes to representing grass. There are some commercially prepared grasses available at the hobby

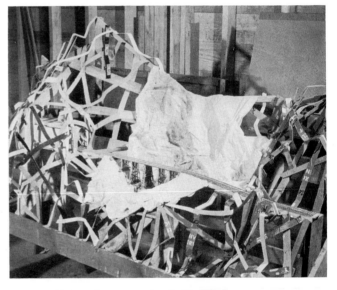

4-33 Jack Work created the scene shown in color in fig. 8-1 by these stages. Grid frame was built on a slope rather than level to begin with. Roadbed was supported as usual on risers, with a depressed board to support trestle. Support for scenic terrain was built up by hodgepodge of cardboard strips and covered with several layers of 6″ x 10″ scraps of paper towels dipped in spackling compound. Additional thickness was added later with texture paint wherever more strength or a base for rock carving was needed. After the trestle was set in place, plastic water and pebbles were arranged in the creek bed. Finally, color, grasses, bushes, and trees were added, as you can see in the color photo.

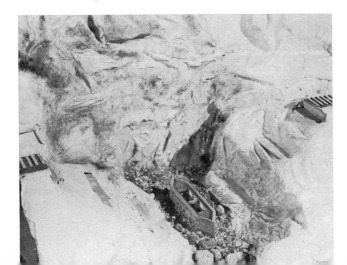

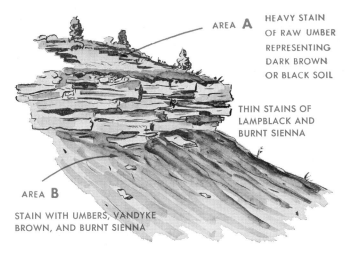

AREA **A**
HEAVY STAIN
OF RAW UMBER
REPRESENTING
DARK BROWN
OR BLACK SOIL

THIN STAINS OF
LAMPBLACK AND
BURNT SIENNA

AREA **B**

STAIN WITH UMBERS, VANDYKE
BROWN, AND BURNT SIENNA

4-34 Coloring limestone outcropping.

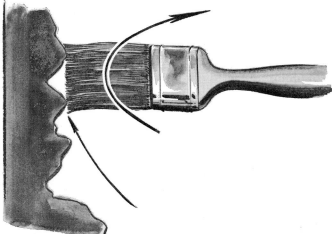

4-35 "Dry brush" just whisks the surfaces.

shops, but most of them are either too green or too even in color. I prefer to dye my own.

Sawdust can be had for the asking at most places where there's a lot of sawing going on. Even at worst, if you happen to encounter some money-mad merchant, a big sack can be had for only a few cents. Most large lumberyards have a lot of saws going, and if you approach the yard manager right, he'll give you all you can carry away. Go to the yard armed with a big paper sack, as it's not too practical to stuff the sawdust in your pockets.

I prefer to sift the sawdust to remove the occasional large chunks and splinters. Then I dye it three or four shades of green, keeping each different color in a separate box. Some folks dye sawdust with oil colors in a turpentine wash. Others use fabric dyes such as Rit, Tintex or the Putnam dyes. These can be mixed in warm water, and as far as I can tell are just as rich and lasting in color as the oil colors.

Let's say you want to use one of the water dyes. Mix a teaspoonful of the dye in a 1-pound coffee tin almost full of water, about 200 degrees. Pour in the sifted sawdust gradually, stirring all the while, until you have a pulpy mass that has absorbed all of the dye solution. Next, spread this pulpy mass of dyed sawdust on enough layers of old newspapers to keep the moisture from seeping through and dyeing the floor, and let it dry in a wind-free

room. After it's dry, store it in an old cigarbox.

It has been standard procedure for years to fix this sawdust grass in place on the layout by sprinkling it over some adhesive material which has been brushed over the plaster area where you want grass. An old flour sifter or a screen-wire strainer makes an excellent grass sifter. Another method is to take an old coffee can and lid (what would we model railroaders do if it weren't for coffee cans?) and punch fairly large holes in the lid. Load the can with grass and use it like a saltshaker.

In fixing the grass in place, do not use any adhesive that dries with a shine. I know that for years lots of fellows painted their grassy areas with a heavy coat of green enamel or household paint, then sprinkled this with dyed sawdust while the paint was still "tacky." Most of the recognized experts in the scenery business now turn thumbs down on this method. The trouble is, when the loose sawdust that doesn't adhere to the paint is removed with a vacuum cleaner, there are always a few spots of shiny, solid green paint showing through the sawdust.

Casco and Cascamite, glues which are mixed with water, are good adhesives *if they're fresh.* So is Weldwood. However, I've had best results using one of the white glues like Elmer's Glue-All or Fuller's Glue. I thin the glue about 50 percent with water,

brush it on, and sprinkle on the dyed sawdust. Let it dry overnight, brush off the surplus that hasn't stuck, and you have a lasting grassy area. Incidentally, grass that doesn't stick can be brushed back into the box and used again.

Use a little judgment in "sowing" your grass. In areas where the earth obviously would remain damp, sift in the darker greens, but in spots that drain rapidly, leaving the soil dry for long periods, the grass must have a yellow or brownish tinge. Intermediate shades should be sown in between the two extremes.

Grass growing around the edges of ponds and along creek banks is of a rich green shade and more lush than that which is spread over a large, flat, sunbaked surface. Break the monotony of the lush green grass along such damp spots with clumps of shrubs and reeds and a few trees. The more yellow or brownish grass on the dry, sunbaked areas should be splotched with irregular areas of the brown earth showing through.

Don't try to cover too large an area with grass at one time. Brush the adhesive over about 1 square foot of area in an irregular fashion, sift on the sawdust, press it down; then move on and work another section about the same size. If you attempt to cover too large an area all at once, you'll find that your adhesive will soak into the plaster and consequently the sawdust won't stick to it.

5 HARD-SHELL SCENERY

By Linn H. Westcott

BILL has been telling you about the traditional methods of erecting the terrain. What follows in this chapter is not a new method so much as a particular selection of parts of several old techniques combined for convenience and effectiveness.

In reading about the many methods of scenerybuilding and in looking at various layouts you may have come to the same conclusion as I have:

It seems you can build mighty fine scenery with any of a dozen kinds of plaster or other media. And it seems that many methods of going about it are nearly equal in results.

So, is there a best plaster? Is there a best way to use it?

Very little comparative study had been made so far as I could tell. This is understandable. When the first material and method one tries proves satisfactory, why look further?

Well, I'm a curious sort, so I took on the task of buying dozens of kinds of plasters, and trying scores of tech-

niques, just to see what I could learn.

I found there was more difference in plasters than I had suspected. I found that some allow you to do much better work than others. Fortunately, the plaster that seems to be the most versatile for expert work is also cheap and practical for ordinary work also.

In studying techniques, I found a combination of other men's ideas that produces good-looking scenery very quickly. It is so practical and easy to use that I hope many model railroaders who have shunned scenery will now try it. It is also easy to use to make parts of existing scenery look better with only minutes of work. I divide the system into three parts:

● **Hard-shell terrain.** This is a very thin shell of a special plaster so strong it is self-supporting and needs no wire screen. In fact, I use it in place of screen and then add a layer of ordinary plaster over the hard shell for finishing the scenery. Construction is fast.

● **Zip texturing.** This is a method of adding plaster, dyes, and dry coloring materials over the hard shell in such a way that very natural scenic effects are produced almost automati-

cally in the right places. The result is effective stratified rock (or igneous type, if you prefer), loose soil that isn't really loose but looks it, and grass. Part of the zip terrain process produces rivulets by actual erosion with water, in such a way that the whole effect is enhanced. Zip terrain construction goes even faster than the hard shell that supports it.

The combination of zip texturing over hard shell could be considered as permanently finished scenery. However, it is not the ultimate.

● **Scenic detailing.** As effective as zip texturing is, the very fact that it is semiautomatic in application means that it will produce a limited variety of effects. All of us are striving for realism in our railroad scenes, and there are many things you can do on top of zip-textured terrain to make it even more realistic. I'm thinking of the advantages of adding rock castings, simulating water, making more effective foliage, making rocks look even more true to life, and the like.

Speed or superdetail?

Unfortunately, really detailed scenery takes lots of time. I have spent

5-1 Scenery in all stages of construction on the Sunset Railway & Navigation Co.

48 hours of modeling time on one cliff only 2 feet long. This takes more patience than many model railroaders may have, or at least more time than they care to spend. Fortunately, a model railroad can look much better than average without any detailing. Just the hard shell plus zip texturing will do it nicely.

And if you are really in a hurry, you can even eliminate the zip texturing. This is an idea for a club getting ready for a public show, for instance, or for a dealer wanting to erect a display quickly. Just build the hard-shell terrain, spray it with dye and sprinkle with grass as explained in the next chapter, and a small railroad scene is made very attactive in only a few minutes.

This chapter tells all about hard-shell terrain and the next tells about zip texturing. Scenery detailing data is located in several places throughout the book.

Now let's get on to the materials and tools needed for hard-shell terrain: see fig. 5-2.

Materials

Hydrocal: Get the "Industrial white" grade of this product if you can, or another grade if that's all there is. This is made by U. S. Gypsum Co. After several years of its popularity in model railroading, no exact substitute has yet been reported. Hydrocal is sold by lime and cement dealers, also by suppliers to the pattern-making industry. A 100-pound bag will cost a little over $5 and will prepare about 50 square feet of terrain. Some hobby shops repackage it in smaller quantities. As this material is not available in some areas, "molding plaster" of the gypsum type (available almost everywhere) can be substituted; but for strength you may have to use two layers of it where the story calls for one.

Paper towels: Prefer a variety that will not tear easily when wet. I used Scott's UHA as sold to industrial plants and office building maintenance departments. The same make sold in retail stores seemed to be inferior, but I could be wrong. Prefer the folded sort because you can tear it or saw whole blocks of it into small pieces conveniently.

The towels will be used for dipping into plaster and then applying to the scenic area.

Newspapers: You need a big pile of these.

Masking tape: In ½" or ¾" width.

Wood sticks: Provide a supply of 1 x 1 sticks cut from 6" to as long as the height of your proposed hill or mountains. You'll need no more than one stick for each 4 square feet of scenery surface.

Wood screws: 1¼-8 flathead steel. These are used to attach the posts to your framework or tabletop. Two per post will be ample.

Tools

Water vessels: I like to keep three 1-gallon plastic pails on hand. One contains a supply of clean water for mixing into plaster; another has water for rinsing tools and hands. The third pail is used for a small supply of the dry Hydrocal plaster.

Mixing vessel: This is for mixing the plaster. It should be at least 7" long. A Pyrex bread pan is fine because it is rectangular and deep. Any Pyrex glass vessel is particularly easy to clean of plaster at any time.

Measuring cups: Again prefer Pyrex to metal or plastic because plaster doesn't cake on it. As a minimum, get a 1-cup measure. However, it is nice to have three: one for dry plaster, one for water, and a 1-quart measure for big batches. This last will be handier in the zip terrain work than in this hard-shell support making, so it doesn't appear in fig. 5-2.

Rubber cake-mixing spatula: I give mine a spray coat of lacquer every once in a while to keep plaster from sticking to it.

If plaster does cake on any of your tools, soak them overnight (or several days if necessary) in water, changing the water occasionally. The plaster dissolves slowly but can be removed eventually. Likewise, plaster poured into drains will not clog them as long as you make sure to run water through for at least a half minute after dumping each leftover batch of scrapings into the drain. However, don't put big chips down the drain.

Garment bags: One or more plastic garment or shirt bags from the laundry are excellent to spread over track and structures so plaster spatters and dust will not get on your railroad. These can be used many times over.

Basic procedure

We are going to put posts up in the area to be covered with scenery; then we'll attach a web of masking tape between post tops. To this web we'll attach wads and sheets of newspaper to make a full-size mockup of the scenery shape.

At this point we inspect it for shape and location. While corrections can easily be made later, this is the first chance we have to see if the hills, ravines, and other scenic details are where we want them and are of the right height.

Then we mix plaster, dip towel scraps into it, and lay the scraps over the newspaper wads. Soon the entire mockup of scenery has a thin plaster covering. In only an hour it is so hard that you can pull the newspapers and tape out from under. Reinforcement is then added with extra layers selectively located, and the job is ready to apply zip texturing.

With this program the hard shell really replaces the screen wire of some other methods. Hard shell is not finished scenery any more than screen wire is. It is just an easier way to erect support.

Let us assume that you have some idea where you want hills and valleys to go, and how high you want them. Since hard-shell scenery is so easy to make, don't worry about future changes. Put in some good scenery now, if for no other reason than to set off the railroad and prevent trains from falling to the floor if derailed.

Photos by Linn H. Westcott except as indicated.

5-2 Simple tools and equally simple materials are all that are needed for the hard-shell support.

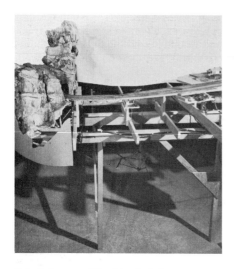

5-3 I began with this L-girder construction, but the very same scenery methods can be used above flat plywood tablework.

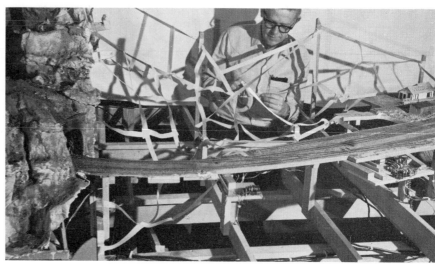

5-4 It took me less than 20 minutes to raise the supporting posts and string this masking-tape web.

The hard shell and zip texturing method goes so fast that if you ever want the scenery arranged differently, it won't take long to replace any part of it. In a way, this brings the same flexibility to scenery that sectional track does to track arrangement changes.

Erecting the posts

The 1 x 1 posts are fastened to the joists or tabletop with one or two screws each. At this time do not put them closer than 18" to 24". You can see in fig. 5-4 how few are needed. I know you will be skeptical about the ultimate strength of this self-supporting shell of plaster, but it is not yet time to worry about it. Get the shell erected first; then you can strengthen it where necessary, either by adding more posts or, as I most usually do, by thickening it. I'll tell you more about this later.

The advantage of not putting posts closer than 18" at this stage is in the ease of erecting and arranging the mockup. That's just as important now as strength will be later.

In most cases, erecting the posts wherever the joists in the framework happen to be is adequate (fig. 5-5). Make each post rise up to about the level where you expect the final scenery surface above each joist to be. If you aren't sure, allow a little extra height. You can lop off the top of a post at any future time.

You may be tempted to put posts where the peaks of mountains and troughs of valleys will go, but this isn't necessary. Peaks and troughs are strongly self-supporting. Usually it is simplest to merely erect posts 18" to 24" apart at convenient places regardless of the scenery shaping planned between support points. See fig. 5-5.

The mockup

With the posts in place, spin a web of masking tape between posts, attaching the tapes about 1" below the post tops (fig. 5-4). This web need not follow the future contours of the proposed scenery unless convenient, but it should generally be a little below the level of the proposed earth surfaces.

An exception is in a proposed ravine (fig. 5-6). Here the web will be above the eventual surface, and another tape can be hung from it like a catenary. The midair tape will be ripped out after the hard shell has become self-supporting.

Next, use wads, rolls, cones, pads, smooth sheets, crumpled sheets, and any other shapes of newspaper or towel you find convenient to build a full-size, in-place mockup of the proposed scenery. If the paper is too springy to stay where I want it, I spray it with water (fig. 5-7). Dry

5-5 Your existing crossbrace or joist spacing will probably be adequate for erecting supporting posts. Too many posts would be a nuisance and not necessarily the best way to increase strength.

5-6 Wads of paper, shown gray, are easily attached above the tapes to develop the desired level and sloping parts of the terrain-to-be. Heavy color shows the position of the tape web itself.

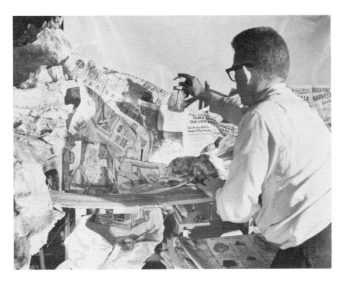

A. L. Schmidt.

5-7 In just a few minutes the newspaper mockup can be attached to the masking-tape web. I had to wet the paper at one place to make it lie close to the web: it tended to spring too high. The water did the trick.

5-8 On a flattop model railroad table, supporting posts are not necessary. Merely use wads of paper or anything else that's convenient to build up the desired shape of the hill. Tape the wads in place; then cover them with plaster-soaked toweling.

newspaper will attach directly to the tape web. Wet pieces can be wrapped with a piece of tape all around and then the wrapper tape can be attached to a web tape.

At this point you can stand back and see your scenery beginning to form. It might be a good idea to leave it overnight and look at it with a fresh viewpoint tomorrow, but not if the evening is still young, because you can make alterations at any time later. Rechecking before adding the shell is merely a suggestion.

I have another suggestion. It is not too easy to judge the shape of the scenery if you use sheets with photos and black advertisements or funny papers in the top layer. So save the classified ads or else — and this is *deluxe* — add a wet layer of paper towels over the newspapers at this time. This has the advantage of letting you study the scenery shaping without the camouflage of newspaper printing.

At places you may want to lower the mockup surface. This is easily done by breaking a tape near a post and using a short piece spliced on to attach the broken web tape lower on the post. To raise any area, more layers of paper pads can be added.

Mountains versus knolls

It is very easy to model rugged mountains, because wads of newspapers naturally take on the general shaping of craggy rocks. Nearly flat land, also low hilly terrain such as the rolling hills of Los Angeles, or England, or Wisconsin, take just a little more time, because you have to fill-in the cavities. Laying on strips of wetted newspaper helps produce a smoothed covering before the plaster comes.

Another technique is to erect a temporary shelf of cardboard or plywood, something like the right-hand side of fig. 5-6 but not permanent and not necessarily large or level. Often a sling of tape will be sufficient support for these temporary shelves. Over this surface, sand, mica or rockwool insulation, or any other cheap bulk material, can be shaped along with wads of paper. Next comes a wet paper overlay. The plaster, when applied, will take on the same smooth sandbox shaping you have temporarily modeled here. The undersupport is removed after the plaster sets.

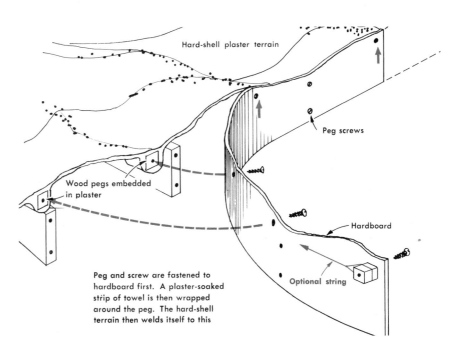

5-9 Ordinary hardboard such as Masonite makes an excellent front board for a model railroad layout because you can easily cut it to rise and fall with the level of the scenery. This construction also anchors it securely to the plaster, yet allows you to remove the board for getting behind it even after the scenery is in place. Start by screwing short 1 x 1 pegs near the top edge of the profile board. Then fasten the profile board to your main framework and add the scenery. When you come to a peg, wrap a piece of plaster-wetted paper towel around it; then add scenery plaster above it. The two will bond together. After the plaster has set, the peg screws can be removed to take the front board off at any time. The profile board and plaster will each strengthen the other. The plaster edge will be stronger if you run a string from peg to peg before adding plaster. This string becomes embedded in the edge of the plaster at a place where it is desirable to have extra strength to prevent chipping.

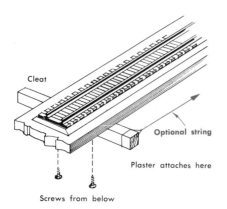

Cleat

Optional string

Plaster attaches here

Screws from below

5-10 Cleats can be screwed under your roadbed material to form outriggers for attaching tape. These cleats will also help support the plaster. String can be run from cleat to cleat to provide the same kind of reinforcement as in fig. 5-9.

5-11 A single layer of hard-shell scenery is very thin but amazingly strong. You really have to try it to believe it. Here is a partly finished hard-shell mound which will be removable but will hide a switch machine on my pike.

The hard shell

Ready? Now comes the making of the hard shell itself. Cover the floor with newspapers, changing them every few hours if plaster accumulates, so you don't track much into the rest of the house. Cover the track and any finished scenery within 4 feet of your work area with garment bags (or several layers of newspapers). Put on old clothes and place a foot-wiping rug at the exit from the room. Be sure you use it!

Start with a small batch of Hydrocal until you get the feel of the operation. Put 1 cup of clean water into the clean bread pan. Then sift (or dump in) 2 cups of Hydrocal. Always put the water in first, as this practically eliminates trouble from lumps or bubbles.

Don't stir until you see the plaster is mostly saturated with water. Make the mix thick enough to stick to both sides of a scrap of towel dipped into the pan. If the plaster runs off so you can see the paper texture, make the mix thicker by adding just a little more plaster. If too thick, thin with more water. The mixture depends to a certain extent on the hardness of your water: the exact ratio for me was 3½ parts plaster by weight to 1 part water, weighed on a baby scale; but this really isn't critical. Now I just guess.

The plaster should harden in from 20 minutes to 1 hour. If the time is too short, read the material on plaster in the next chapter for better understanding of what to do about it. Usually you will have no trouble at all.

Tear the towels into pieces that are convenient for you to handle. I use mostly pieces about 3″ x 6″ or so, but

on a big job you might want much bigger pieces. I find the easiest way to get a scrap, or lamina, of towel covered is to lower it zigzag fashion into the container and make sure both sides are coated as I lift it out.

Slap the first lamina piece on top of a hill or mountain and work down the sides with only a little overlap of each new piece (fig. 5-8). Whenever you come to one of the supporting posts, be sure the plaster-coated towel touches the top of the post; then add a second layer at this point. This will provide a strong, gussetlike supporting point.

The Hydrocal can be manipulated safely for about 15 minutes. After this, leave it alone. In about an hour it will be quite hard but also warm, showing that it is still getting harder. Fresh material can be added to the edges as long as you don't crack the half-hard layers.

Work to cover the area generally. You can go back and close small openings at the end of a batch, using smaller scraps of towel.

A neat way to attach a front board onto the hard shell is shown in fig. 5-9. This allows you to remove the front board to get at wiring or other items. Yet when the profiled board (thin hardboard) is in place, it and the terrain each reinforce the other.

The plaster adheres well on its own to the edges of roadbed, but I do provide a cleat a little wider than the roadbed itself here and there to give extra support (fig. 5-10).

If you have an overhanging cliff, build the top and bottom first; then add the overhanging part last. It will usually stay in place nicely.

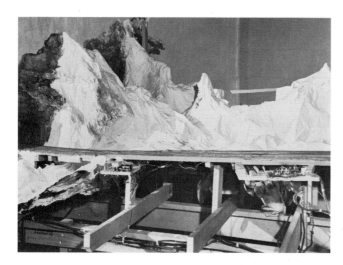

5-12 After a layer of hard shell has been applied, you can stand back and study the scene. Here the mountain peak at far right is too abruptly sharp and the one near center is much too spiked. Note the tape strung from one peak to the other. Had these mountains been satisfactory this tape would now be ripped away. However, it was instead used to build more newspaper and then more terrain in the saddle between the peaks.

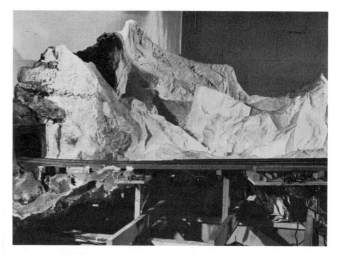

5-13 On a later inspection things were better, but the peak at right was eventually lopped off (see fig. 5-1) with a saber saw passing through plaster and wood together. A lamina or two of plastered towel was then added to re-form the peak more rounded. Posts went into these particular peaks, but, as explained in the text, peaks can be located just as well between posts, as was done in fig. 5-5. I hadn't learned that yet.

Inspection

You will be surprised how hard the thin shell is, even though it may be less than 1/16″ thick at places (fig. 5-11).

Step back and look at the scenery surface. Again you can make corrections to it if you wish. See figs. 5-12 and 5-13. You can saw the hard shell with a pointed saw or a saber saw, or punch through it with a screwdriver. It will usually break or cut only where you want it to, provided the adjacent edges are touching the roadbed, the table front board, or a post .

Watch out at this point for grotesque mountain peaks, or too many of any unusual features, unless you know enough about geology to make them really convincing.

It can pay to take 5 minutes to sprinkle a little diluted dye on the hard shell just to help you visualize the shape. This will also make it look like rock instead of plaster in case you will be leaving it this way for a while.

Make concentrated solutions of Rit dye in pint jars, using warm water. These are stock solutions. Make them of black and ecru or cocoa brown. Take a little of each color to make separate batches, more diluted, and splash, spray, or sprinkle the dyes on the hard shell after wetting it. The hard shell will take on a rock color which will give you a much better idea of its true shape.

Alterations

Wherever you want the terrain to be higher, add wads of newspaper or towel right on top of the first hard shell and then add more hard-shell laminas. When you want to lower the surface, you can do either of two things: you can saw out the plaster, suspend it at a lower level or slope, and patch the adjoining cracks and openings with fresh laminas; or you can punch out a part of the original hard shell entirely, suspend newspapers from a tape sling in the newly desired conformation, and then add a new hard shell.

Watch out for hollows where water can collect in ponds. The hard shell is sufficiently waterproof that you can find these places by pouring water right onto the surface. While hollows do occur in nature, they usually look unnatural on a model unless you know how to treat them by making them into ponds, swamps, or sinkholes. Generally you want to provide natural-looking outlets to "drain" them. The bottoms of such watercourses follow the levels shown dashed in fig. 5-14.

Reinforcement, if needed

After the surface is satisfactory, remove all the tape and newspaper you can reach from underneath. It really isn't needed and it's a potential fire hazard anyway. I've mentioned that the hard shell is thin yet amazingly strong at this stage. Fig. 5-11 shows a single layer partly covering a switch machine. This is all the thickness you need in a small mound, or in parts of the scenery in ravines or on mountaintops.

Why is it so strong? Actually it is rock. It is alabaster, a very hard form of gypsum (calcium sulfate). It is so tightly bonded that it doesn't soak up color or paint nearly as well as plasters of the usual sort. That's one of several reasons a different kind of plaster will be used later for the finishing and detailing.

Despite the great strength and self-supporting qualities of the hard shell, you don't want to risk someone putting nearly his full weight near the edge of the table, so some reinforcing is in line.

Put a lamp under the scenery and then darken the room. See fig. 5-15. Note that light shows through most of the alabaster rock. This test helps you locate any openings or very thin places. Slap another lamina of Hydrocal over each weak spot.

Usually, mountainous surfaces are very strong because of their irregularity, so only the places where light comes through quite brightly need be covered. Smoother hills and plains may need somewhat more thickness: perhaps so very little light shows through.

Next add an extra layer around all the outer edges and along the sides of the track and at places where visitors might lean on their elbows. The shell might take it, but two layers are four times as strong as one, so let's be safe.

When you apply any added coats, first wet the lower coat with water. Let plenty soak in so the first coat doesn't rob water from the second. Gypsum won't set if it dries in less than an hour. If it begins to dry be-

5-14 As you build your scenery you will find there is a tendency for the terrain to produce pockets or hollows in the more-level areas. These will not look natural if you leave them as they are. You can eliminate the pockets either by making sure each has a ravine or swale as an outlet (dashed line) or by filling them with earth to make small meadows. If suited to the land you are modeling, some pockets can be turned into ponds, swamps, or sinkholes. You can locate the depressions that need such attention simply by pouring water over the hard-shell surface and watching where it collects.

5-15 Thin places in the hard-shell terrain are easy to find simply by placing a light underneath it. The shell is actually rock — that's why it's so hard — but it is so pure you can see light through it. For more strength, add more plaster-soaked towel.

5-16 Scenery can be extended beyond the edge of the table for any purpose. Here it was erected temporarily to provide foreground for a photo. Temporary ledges can be built alongside any tracks to act as engine catchers until the permanent scenery can be designed and installed.

5-17 Arapaho Creek comes down the right branch in this view. An old channel lies slightly higher to the left. The old channel was built first.

5-18 When the new channel was built, the side of the old channel (here held in position) was saved in case I decided to return to the original arrangement.

fore setting, add water. The setting process will revive, so no harm is done.

If you can't locate Hydrocal

If you use molding plaster because you have no Hydrocal on hand, you will probably want more thickness. This is easy. First lightly dye-color the surface; then add a second layer of paper towels soaked in plaster all over. The dye merely helps you find areas not yet double-covered. Two layers of molding plaster are a little stronger than one layer of Hydrocal.

For extra strength where needed

If you want to walk on the scenery, you don't need posts much closer together, but you do need a still stronger shell. Cut scraps of plastic window screen, dip them in Hydrocal, and build a second layer over the first. Overlap the screen pieces just a little. Being imbedded, this screen should give better support than screen used in the usual way. Gauze could also be used for strong scenery as a second — or even in a first — coat.

Plaster surgery and place lifting

Under "Alterations" I mentioned that you can add new scenery above old scenery or cut out a part of the shell and build it anew. I also mentioned that you could cut out a piece of the scenery and reweld it at a new level, at a new slope, or somewhere other than where it came from. All this is very easy.

When putting old work in new locations, wet the edges of the old material so a better bond will be formed. Use a bead of Hydrocal to seal a crack, or add laminas from above or below for extra strength or to seal a gap. Pieces can be suspended with tape or supported on paper until the beads or

splices harden. Then the welds can be concealed by a little zip texturing over the boundaries, as we'll see in the next chapter. The result is, you can't tell where the old work and the new are joined.

All this makes for some advantages one should not overlook. Here are just a few examples:

One of the problems of a new layout is the possibility of trains going to the floor. It is easy to add about 6" of scenery to each side of the roadbed soon after track is laid, whether or not you are ready for final scenerywork. If this temporary 6" safety strip happens to be at the wrong level or slope when it comes time for final work, alter it or

5-19 A small slot was sawed through the scenery shell to locate the edges of the "excavation" needed for placing the bridge. Later the entire riverbed under the track was removed but was saved to be replaced. Cutting this slot ensured that I did not remove too much of the adjoining scenery. Patching later was easy.

bash it out and replace it. Neither the cost nor the time taken to erect it is great, and meanwhile you will never know how many locomotive pilots you have saved by installing this safety strip in the first place.

Fig. 5-17 shows Arapaho Creek where it comes through an arch bridge on my Sunset Ry. The main channel branches to the right. In floodtime the left just might get water. This divided stream effect is found in real life, but it came about by chance on my Sunset Ry. Originally the creek flowed through the left-hand channel. After the arch bridge was installed, my younger son Russell suggested that the new channel to the right might add interest. I sawed out the side of the old creekside to try out the idea; I saved the piece so it could go back if I didn't like the new way. See fig. 5-18. After the new channel was in place, I decided to keep it that way. The old channel at the left could have been covered over, but it is a convenient site for a quartz rock quarry that was planned for somewhere in this ravine.

The bridge itself involved some surgery to the scenery. The bridge was made as a separate project; then the riverbed at the bridgesite was sawed out (fig. 5-19). After the bridge was installed, the old riverbottom piece was trimmed to fit and was welded back into its original place. Since the riverbottom was the same piece that had been removed to accept the bridge, it was a perfect fit to the adjoining creekbed when rewelded into place.

The quarry spur was planned from the beginning. Originally it was to pass under the right side of the arch and continue on a steep grade up to the middle of the photo; see fig. 5-20. It was to swing a little to the right be-

48

hind the creamery and join the last track of middistant Anachrona Yard. The river route was planned with this track route in mind.

Well, after the ravine of Swiss Fork was built, I could see that the spur would make a much more interesting feature if it crossed the fork, ran along the cliffside a little beyond the arch, then recrossed near the yard. Such a route can be justified because this new route will leave more space for higher-level industries in the area where the original low-level track would have had to be.

If this quarry spur track had been built first, as originally planned, the better route might not have been thought of. And if it had been thought of, it would be more work to rebuild. By building the scenery first, this spur will be a much better attraction.

Some snow-blasted peaks I built nearly a year ago now seem to me to be too close to the table front, but I can easily saw them out of their present location and move them, still attached to their supporting posts, to a better location farther back. If new posts are needed, they can easily be welded to any point underneath any part of the hard-shell scenery.

Even if I have to move away, some of my scenery can be sawed out and saved. Thus it will pay me to spend more time on detailing parts of it.

I'm not one to enter model contests, but if a modeler wanted to, he could saw out a part of his pike — scenery, track, and all — and take it to a contest. When he came home, he could hang the prize ribbon on the wall and put the scenery and track back in place. Splicing does not take long. I proved it.

How about access pits and hatches? Maybe we don't need as many with hard-shell scenery. It's so easy to cut a hole and then put the piece back that the only hatches needed should be for daily access, not for infrequent re-

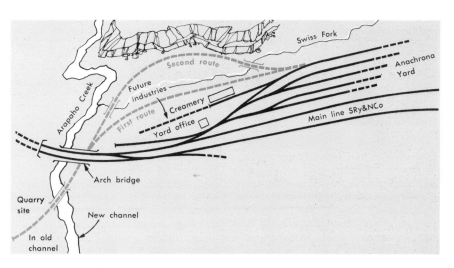

5-20 A proposed quarry spur will take the opposite bank of Swiss Fork, thus permitting more industries to use the high-level land near the creamery. For a photo of this scene, see fig. 5-1.

pairing. I have even welded a former access hatch shut.

I must add one more facet to this polygon of scenery techniques. Traditionally a man waited until all track was laid and working well before building any scenery. Then, particularly for large layouts, the idea of building scenery a little at a time developed. Bill McClanahan mentions this in chapter 2. A step further is to build the scenery before the track, as is evidenced by a photo of John Allen's layout: fig. 2-19.

But with hard-shell terrain, not only is it possible to build the track after the scenery (if strong enough, the hard shell can even be the track support, but that's beside the point of what I'm getting at), but also the planning of the mainline routes themselves can be done after scenery already exists. With hills, valleys, cliffs, lakes, rivers, towns, and roads already in place, the construction of a model railroad through "existing" terrain will have to solve the same problems the real roads had to solve when they

were built. The way you solve these location problems is going to add much interest to the railroad and produce a more convincing layout scene. The railroad will be engineered to the terrain instead of the scenery being contrived to fit the track.

This idea is only slightly practical for the very crowded or small pike, but when you have a little more space to work in, so track can be shifted left or right a little (or rising and falling), when finally located it can be at its best.

The ease of removing parts of the hard shell and then putting the material back in its place eliminates any major problems of the clumsiness of working scenery-first. Also, if you really don't want the track to go so far to the left to skirt a cliff, you can move the cliff a little instead and it will still look as if the railroad was located through the scenery.

Time will tell how far this idea will get in the hobby. I've begun to do it this way myself and find it a lot of fun. Some others will; some won't.

6 ZIP TEXTURING

By Linn H. Westcott

A NOVICE can build scenic terrain by any of many methods and still get excellent results. The differences in methods are more in convenience, permanence, weight, and simplicity than in effect. Both the clumsy and the easy methods can produce good-looking terrain.

But scenery-shaping is only part of the job. Next the surfaces need textures to represent soil, rock, and grass; and they need coloring appropriate to these materials. Again, there are many methods, but this time most methods require an experienced hand. Only a few techniques are so nearly automatic that they will produce good results for a novice. This chapter, then, is devoted to suggesting a combination of techniques which almost without effort produce natural-looking rock, soil, and grass. The work progresses so quickly that, with tongue in cheek, I have called it "zip texturing." Perhaps it should be explained that the program was introduced at about the time the U. S. Post Office introduced its "zip code" numbers.

Starting with white or tinted plaster terrain, you can have several square feet of your scenery looking quite realistic in only minutes. (You can also do zip texturing over existing scenery you are not satisfied with.)

One time a friend came to see my layout after having been away about a year. One of his first remarks was: "That scenery must have taken hours and hours to do." Well, there is one place where only 2 feet of my scenery did take many hours to detail, but fortunately for my act he wasn't referring to that. He was looking at the bulk of the scenery around Arapaho Creek. This consists of some level ground, some ravines and slopes, and several rocky cliffs with mossy effects, tufts of grass in the crevices, and loose soil trapped on ledges. This part looks reasonably realistic but it took very little time to do. The texturing and coloring took less than an hour; and I told him so. See inside front cover.

He didn't believe it, so I went over to a little box and brought back a water-filled window sprayer, a spoon, a kitchen sieve, and a jar containing some olive-green powder — actually a mixture of dry plaster and green dry powder pigment.

In 10 seconds I had about 2 square feet of previously uncolored scenic terrain wetted with the sprayer. In another 10 seconds I had sifted color over the surface. The scenery immediately looked finished. There are more steps to the whole process, but this quick demonstration shows the principle and how simple and nearly automatic it is. The grass dust (which looks more like grass than sawdust does) covers the level places and ledges almost completely, but on the sheer faces of cliffs it hardly shows. What little does cling to the steeper slopes tends to bring out the rocky shape of the terrain in a very natural way. It looks more like moss on the rocks than grass.

Soil can be made and applied the same way. Usually it should be applied before adding grass, but I took a shortcut for my demonstration to save about 20 seconds.

Well, I had my man convinced, as I did likewise with a number of my friends on other visits. They write that they are enjoying the scenery-work, and the results as well. I realize that the colors in a reproduction are never the same as in the original. So I suppose the greens and earth colors of that inside cover and page 54 may be distorted. But at least fig. 6-8 will show you how grass clings differently at different places. So does soil. All the coloring and earth and rock grain effects shown were added over hard-shell terrain by this zip texturing method, except for the tunnel portal and bridge masonry. These were painted with dyes.

A natural method

The principal reason this zip texturing looks realistic and is so easy to do is that it comes close to the way real coloring occurs in nature.

Loose soil and grass occur in nature on all level surfaces unless wind, water, or traffic wear them away faster than they accumulate. Soil and greenery also cleave to ledges, crevices, and other irregularities in rock, but fall away from sheer faces.

By combining the dusting-on principle with a washing-away principle, earth and grass colors will deposit and wash away from the model terrain almost exactly as they do in real life. Therefore, if one chooses proper colors and doesn't overdo it, the result just *has* to look natural. Automatic as it is, it is also naturally correct.

But zip texturing has its limitations. The result of doing an entire railroad with zip-textured scenery will compare favorably with much of the scenery you see on model railroads today. The limitation comes when you want something still better. The trouble with zip texturing as it comes is that it is all one similar effect.

I consider zip texturing of value in two ways. First, it turns a jumble of L-girders, stilts, midair track, and a jungle of wires into a presentable, finished-looking railroad scene. Second, it makes a good base on which to do detailed scenery sometime later, at one's leisure.

Zip-textured scenery should, of course, be enhanced by the addition of foliage fairly soon. Later, rock castings, stone walls, roads, paths, simulated water effects, cattle trails, piles of rocks at field edges, plowed areas, abandoned gravel pits and the like can be added for more interest. These details will also make the model layout seem bigger.

Tools

Want to try zip texturing? If so, the biggest part of the work will be done when you have gathered the tools and materials. Keep them handy at all times and it will never be a problem to touch up little places here and there

6-1 In addition to the plaster-mixing tools illustrated in chapter 5, the tools circled here are the most-used for zip texturing. The unmarked tools are used for more detailed scenerywork not described in this chapter. The syringe is an alternative for the modified squeeze bottle at upper left. Extra brush sizes are handy but are rarely essential. Firm bristles on small brushes are preferable.

6-2 Some of these photos illustrate the left bank at the foot of Arapaho Creek on my Sunset Ry. Old scenery, left, has been extended with hard-shell base to a recently installed hardboard front board. Any resemblance of the new work to real rock is accidental except for arranging the shapes of newspaper wads that formed the temporary undersupport.

6-3 Since the plaster had to be wetted anyway for the following techniques, I added dye to color the hard shell. This helped in bringing out the shaping as I worked. Also, should an upper layer be chipped away, it will prevent white from showing. I applied dye water generously. A bucket on the floor caught the overflow from the bottom of the stream.

and anywhere as your railroad grows. For instance, when a new structure is installed you can have the earth, grass, and roadway around it in place in minutes, rather than waiting for the next time you decide to build scenery.

One caution: if you have track with flexible fiber ties such as the older type of Atlas flexible track, keep water away from these ties. You can drench plastic and wood ties as much as you want without damage, but fiber ties will warp if wet. The danger is eliminated if you lay strips of plastic garment bags or something similar over the roadbed area whenever spraying with water or dusting-on colors.

Here are the tools. Those not already shown in the previous chapter can be seen in fig. 6-1.

● Set of kitchen sieves including both coarse and medium mesh.

● Measuring cup or cups.

● Measuring spoons, stainless preferred.

● Syringe, or modified squeeze spray bottle for directing a stream of water. Spray bottle nozzle can be pulled out and modified so all water comes through draw tube.

● One or several sprayers. Prefer a type that sprays much water with little effort but doesn't dribble nor spatter. Jar type, upper left in fig. 6-1, was poor but workable. Window cleaner type, top center, was much better. Of two makes, the one with opaque pump chamber worked better than one with transparent chamber. Probably there are other makes; trying one before buying a second would be wise.

● Tablespoon.

● Rubber cake-mixer spatula.

● Medicine dropper. Use for applying very small amounts of water or color; also for mixing dyes.

● Several wide-mouth jars, such as are used for peanut butter or instant coffee.

● Several bottles to fit sprayers.

● Pressure-sensitive labels. Use these to identify material in containers and to record formulas for earth and grass mixes.

Materials

● **Plaster.** The basic ingredient for most of the zip texturing will be molding plaster. (See the accompanying reference material on scenery plas-

ters.) This is sold by lime and cement dealers. If you don't want to buy 100 pounds of plaster, which costs around $2 to $3, you can use plaster of paris from a drug or hardware store. However, this is often not as finely ground. Patching plaster can also be used, but the built-in retarder may make it work too slowly and may affect dye coloring. Do not let glue or other organic chemicals contaminate your plaster or the water you mix it into.

● **Dry color.** Dry pigments for mixing into plaster can be purchased from large paint stores, or can be ordered through them.

I use the six colors listed in the accompanying data on plaster mixing, page 59. You will want a jar for each color batch you mix and store dry. If you have more bottles, it will be convenient to store your stock of dry pigment in them as well.

Incidentally, I found that a good way to record what a color or mixture will do is to sift a little onto a slab of wet hard plaster and keep it as a color chip. If I remember to label the slab and the jar (and put the formula on the jar), I can always tell not only what the color will do but also how

6-4 French's Gulch on John Allen's Gorre &
Daphetid RR. shows coloring to represent
weathering of bridges and trains as well as
the scenery. Note water flowing from pipes at
upper left.

to mix it again when the supply runs
out.

● **Fluid dye colors.** I'm very pleased
with dyes for coloring rock and for
darkening or modifying pigment colors after they are in place. Rit, Tintex,
or similar dyes are used. These are
the colors I find most handy:

Black.   Yellow.
Cocoa brown.   Green.

The green is used only to neutralize
black or cocoa brown if it gets pinkish.
Yellow has many uses; it is another
way to neutralize any tendency for
black to get pinkish.

At first I was wary of using dye, as
it is not permanent like pigments.
However, I asked friends, and several
had dye-colored scenery that had
lasted for years. It seems to bleach
only if in direct sunlight. Sometimes
retarder or another chemical will
cause lightening when dye is applied
for the first time.

But dye has many virtues. Color in
the plaster, and color painted on, are
very unrealistic because they have no
variation — looking more like ice
cream than rock. But color applied
with dye is much more satisfactory
because it soaks in more here, less
there, in a manner much more like the
natural coloring of rock. Dye can be
mixed into plaster too (sometimes in-
terfering with setting, however), but
dye is at its best when sprayed or
dribbled onto wetted finished scenery
surfaces. Then little streams of dye
find the rills and darken them more
than the jutting points in a most natural manner. Dye darkens a rough
surface more than a smooth one, and
it darts along cracks and grooves to
enhance strata or other textured surfaces. It can be applied over many
times to alter or darken the color. Be
sure to try it. Dye is usually used
quite diluted, but this depends on the
particular dye. Take it easy until you
are sure. It is easy to get much too
strong a coat of black or cocoa brown.

Don't buy gray dye: diluted black
is more natural. If you want a permanent gray that won't ever lighten,
even with bleach, use 32 drops of india
ink in a pint of water. Coffee and tea
(either regular or instant versions)
also make good rock coloring. Tea
tends to be a little pinkish, but a trace
of yellow dye over it brings the color
back to a natural shade.

Dye is very easy to control. Put all
the grains of a package of dye into a
pint bottle and add warm water. This
will make a saturated solution with
some undissolved grains at the bot-

6-5 After wetting the surface a thin coat of molding plaster is brushed over the terrain. Here all brushing is in one direction to simulate shale or sandstone. It is usually best to work from the top gradually downward in all coatings and to overlap onto old completed scenery.

6-6, at right: Diluted household dye is sprayed over the still-wet plaster coating. (Rewet it if it has dried.) Successive coats of diluted black (for a light gray), diluted brown, and yellow dye produce better results than using only one dye color. It is important to keep the coloring fairly light.

6-7 The surface is again wetted and a mixture of earth-colored dry plaster is dusted onto all level and sloping areas. A small amount also clings to cliff sides and helps emphasize their shaping. Moisture from the plaster below soaks upward into this dusty coating to set it in place.

6-8 In exactly the same way rewetted surfaces are dusted with olive-green plaster to simulate grass in a very effective manner. The same level and sloping areas are covered; but unless the region is lush, a little of the earth color should show through the grass coat, especially at the edges.

tom. You can keep adding water as needed yet always know the dye is the same strength as long as there are extra, undissolved grains down there. You can even pour leftover diluted dye back into the stock bottle and it will soon become concentrated.

By measuring out so many medicine droppersful of concentrated dye to a given amount of wetted water, you can always get a working dilution of the same strength. Shake the stock bottle a little before using yellow dye.

Wet plaster takes dye moderately. Dry plaster soaks it up fast — usually too fast.

● **Bleach.** A drop or two of Clorox (or other perchlorate bleach) in about 2 ounces of water provides plenty of bleach for whitening an area previously colored with dye. Use the medicine dropper to apply this to the scenery. An interesting effect, not a part of zip texturing so much as of final detailing, occurs when you let bleach run down from a crevice in rock. It will create the effect of lime deposits on the rock, as though seeping water sometimes evaporated there.

Bleach has no effect on most of the dry pigments, so you can get interesting effects by combining pigment color and dye color, plus some speckles (or even floods) of bleach in localized areas. This is fun to experiment with.

● **Flock.** Grass effects can be enhanced by using flock. Flock consists of short bits of rayon (the best) or other fibers that are meant to be dusted onto a glue-coated surface to give the effect of felt. It sells in 1- and 2-pound packages at sign, display, and some art stores. Walthers also has it in small quantities. If you have a choice, prefer fibers of .030″ length in a waterproof variety. At least get green, although I find a mix of equal parts of green, brown, and yellow handy as explained later. The brand I purchased is Cellusuede, made by the Cellusuede Products Company of Rockford, Illinois. I found it at a local art and display store. It comes in 2-pound bags — and that's an awful lot of flock.

Warning! When using flock, be very sure to put a cloth or some sort of mask across your nose so that you do not breathe in any of the flock fibers. They tend to float in the air for a little while and can be quite damaging to inner tissues of the body if inhaled.

● **Adhesive.** Almost all earth and grass mixes will contain a good deal of dry plaster, since it takes a lot of plaster to make a little pigment lighter in shade. This plaster also serves to hold the mixture onto the terrain permanently, once it sets. The trick, then, is to be sure the dusted-on colors don't get dry for about an hour, long enough for setting to harden them in

place. Saturating the terrain with water beforehand is essential. If a booster spray of water mist must also be used later to avoid drying out too soon, do it carefully so the rewetting doesn't wilt the dust and spoil its loose effect.

Flock, too, can be mixed with plaster to hold it in place, and dry color can be added to kill a too-bright green. The major problem here is that a sieve tends to let plaster and color through and hold the flock back, so a coarse mesh is needed.

Sometimes you want to use flock raw on a surface. For this, a prespraying of gum arabic in water will make the surface tacky. Gum arabic is cheap when bought in dry form from art or drug stores; it costs a little more when bought as a solution. If you can't find a store that has gum arabic, dimestore mucilage can be substituted. All these are diluted, a little thinner than syrup, for spraying. Clean lacquer or varnish can also be used for holding flock.

● **Dulling agent.** Flock is too shiny when applied directly in quantity. A brief spray coat from a self-spray can of Testor's Dullcote, Walthers' DDV, or other matte varnish or lacquer will control the effect. Similarly, glossy lacquer or varnish can increase the

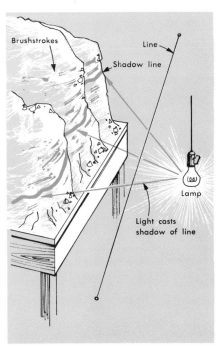

6-9 The shadow of a clothesline is reasonably practical for determining the slope of strata through irregular terrain. In practice the line should be hung as far from the scenery as the room will permit. For tilted strata (a fine effect), tilt the line or place it very high or very low in the room. Once the line is located, only the lamp bulb (or other light) may be moved up and down to create parallel shadows on the terrain at whatever level the modeler is working. Do not disturb the line itself.

sheen of rocks and other effects.

Warning! Do not apply any varnish or lacquer over scenery until all traces of water have dried; then give it a little more drying time. Otherwise an unsightly white bloom may develop under the spray coat.

● **Wetting agent.** Almost all the water used in zip texturing should have a little wetting agent in it to help it wet surfaces, penetrate, and soak quickly into dry materials. A few drops of Liquid Ivory detergent per quart of water does a good job for me. Other brands probably will work as well. Do *not* use wetting agent in the water for mixing batches of plaster or Hydrocal. Do use wetting agent for sprinkling and spraying water on old surfaces to make them ready for new coatings of any kind.

Techniques: the work goes fast

You may already have guessed much of what comes next, but let's discuss the various steps in zip texturing in order. (The order can be changed for various effects.)

● **Wet preparation for each step.** Before almost every operation the surface is first sprayed or sprinkled with wetted water. This helps any plaster, applied either wet or dry, to adhere to the existing surface. It also helps make dye color spread more naturally. If the surface is very dry, give it two coats of wetted water in quick succession before starting the next work.

There are some times when you do not prewet a surface. One is when you want a dye to go on very strongly. Another is when you want to spatter color onto rock, say to get a granite effect.

● **Dye coloring.** If the hard-shell or other terrain is white, you can leave it that way; but usually it is better to spray, brush, swab, or dribble diluted dye onto it to gray it, as in fig. 6-3. Add a little warm color to the black dye: cocoa brown for reddish, cocoa brown plus yellow for a less pinkish tone, or yellow and black alone. Once you find the combination of dye you like, label the formula on the bottle and use it often. You might try this for a start:

2 parts black dye.
1 part cocoa brown dye.
9 parts wetted water.

Note how magically the dye transforms plaster into rocky effects. It tends to bring out irregular shapes and to emphasize cracks. Even hard shell alone, with this dye, makes presentable scenery for a quick job.

If you want darker or varied color, adjust the formula.

Warning! Novices go wrong with scenery coloring more than anything else. Our minds fool us when it comes

6-10 This is a bit of the same scene as in the view on the inside front cover, taken before the arch bridge had been positioned from below. The tunnel portal and the masonry drain leading from it are also made of plaster.

6-11 This fragment of a cliff measures a little over 1 foot long on the Sunset Railway & Navigation Co. layout. It is a blending of rock castings and handwork. Creases that were already in the rock casting seen overhanging at left center were extended by carving across the handmade rockwork to the right. By carrying out the theme and textures already established by the casting, rather than doing something different, the comparatively crude handwork looks almost as good as the naturally made original. By using a wire brush in nearly horizontal direction, the natural crevices of both casting and handwork were deepened, thus increasing the effect of layered rock. A wire brush has this advantage: it deepens crevices going in the direction of brushing more than it cuts the heights. Note the many "joints" extending through the rockwork in several directions as explained in chapter 3. These also help increase realism.

to rock color particularly. Also grass. Rock we think of as gray may in fact be much more of a dirty white. Rock we think of as blackish is, when dry, more often gray or even light gray. So keep colors light, like neutralized (grayed) pastels, when you are coloring rock. Fortunately, dyed rock lightens about the right amount when it dries to correct our wrong impressions; so if you make a mix that looks about right on the rock when wet, it will be nearly correct when dry.

It won't look right yet, but don't add more dye to darken it until you've seen the effect with the zip-textured soil and grass added as I'll soon explain.

Sometimes dyed rock looks a little too pink while still wet. This also tends to correct itself; but if it is still too pink, a little yellow sprayed on will correct it.

You can add correcting sprays of dye to rock after all the soil and grass is in place. These final sprays, if needed, seem to have little effect on the green of the grass.

● **Finished plaster coat.** Your new terrain base — or existing scenery to be recolored — is now given a thin coat of molding plaster. Mix it quite thin, so it just hides the base but not much more. You need it thicker only if you are going to do rock carving.

Should you put color into this batch? A little is all right, but you may not find it worth the bother or risk. The argument for color in plaster is that an accident may chip uncolored plaster and show a garish white blemish. The arguments to the contrary are that it is very easy to dab on a trifle of dye to hide such a blemish: this is certainly less work than mixing-in the color. Also, color in plaster has the risk of being too strong and not easily corrected, and of chemically affecting the setting time. You'll find adherents both ways, but not so much from reason as from habit. A little color in the plaster is a fine idea if you don't mind the extra work. None at all is simpler and produces the same result. You choose. I have done it both ways. If you do use color be sure it is not too dark. You can darken it easily later on. Lightening it is not so easy.

In the accompanying data there is a list of formulas for rock colors. Try one of these for your finish coat. You might increase the amount of plaster a little from the amount shown, perhaps even double it. This won't lighten the color as much as you think, because plaster grains are not as fine as pigment grains, but it will put you on the safer, lighter side. Later, when you get to the earth-dusting step, use the same formula with the normal plaster quantity.

6-12 Rivulets of water are trickled down the hollows of the slope time and time again, washing away the earth layer from bedrock naturally.

6-13 It is easy to hide a switch machine under the removable cap of a small hill or rock outcrop. Saw the cap out of the hard shell and replace it before adding the zip texturing. Then, after zip-texturing, push up from below just enough to break the seal of the new coat. This produces a crack so tiny, visitors never notice it. Disguise edges of larger hatches the same way.

At first only 1 cupful of plaster at a time will be enough, but soon you will know how many cupfuls to mix to suit your own working speed.

Now is the time to make a choice of some importance: whether you want to model "igneous" or "sedimentary" rock. The one is volcanic in origin and the other is the deposit of the sea, rivers, or wind. If you don't know which to choose, I send you here on a pleasant journey back to chapter 3. It's easy reading and now has more meaning for you than it might have had in school.

If you want to represent volcanic rock, put the coat of plaster on fairly wet so that it tends to be smooth. Then, as it sets, stipple it. An easy alternative is to stipple it after it has set hard, adding just a little fresh plaster of the same color. The idea is to get an irregular granular surface but to avoid any points, swirls, or peaks.

I chose the other path for Arapaho ravine: stratified rock. This is done with only a slightly thinner coat, but always brushing in one direction. If you want, you can tie a clothesline somewhere in the other part of the room and hang an extension lamp behind it. See fig. 6-9. Raise or lower the lamp so it casts a shadow of the line near where you are working. Now brush in whatever direction the shadow runs and you'll get a good effect. If the line is about level with the lay-

out and not too close to it, the strata will be the common horizontal sort. But raise or lower one end of the line or both ends and you will get a dipping strata that is particularly interesting in model railroad scenery. Keep the line in the same place once you start, and move only the lamp to cast a shadow higher or lower on your work areas.

Cover all the support with this coat. An exception would be in grottolike stream or cave regions where occasional voids that occur naturally in the new coat need not be closed nor painted over. The pockets may have a very natural effect.

● **Another dye coat.** Another dye coat is now added. This is one reason for having made the previous batch a little light in color. By darkening with dye now, you get a natural variation in color rather than a monotonous flat effect. Spray the dye on (fig. 6-6) or wash it on with a syringe as you prefer. The syringe has the advantage of washing away a little of the surface coating itself (if it hasn't yet hardened), often with most natural results.

In actual practice I usually wash or spray a colored dye on the finished plaster first. A little later I do the same thing with diluted black to make the rocks grayish. The gray immediately makes the rocks take on shape and look old and hard.

Often several other coats are applied. Localized applications of various dyes, thinned more than normally, give color variations that greatly increase the realism.

For special effects, dye can be applied with a medicine dropper over wetted surfaces. For a granite-color effect, flick dye onto a *dry* surface with a toothbrush; or use an airbrush with very, very low pressure so that it spatters small droplets. Do this with several colors and you have the speckled effect of this kind of rock.

Be sure all rock coloring is on the subtle side. You don't need a strong tone to simulate strong color; all colors will look stronger than you think. If the rock is too light after the dye dries, another thin coat can be added.

If you don't need more color at this point, be sure to prewet the surface for the next step.

● **Earth dusting.** In nature, rock is always disintegrating at the surface. Wind also deposits dust on it. This accumulates as soil except where gravity, water, wind, or traffic cleans it away. By dusting dry powdered earth color onto the finished plaster coat, you simulate this effect very well. Use the color of the same chosen formula normal-strength this time. Use a medium-mesh sieve to start, but also try the effect with a coarse mesh. Hold the sieve with one hand and pass it slowly over the entire working area

6-14 A support for the side of this fill was made with hard shell laid over a shirt cardboard cutout. It was then wetted and coated with earth in the same manner as any other scenery. A second coating and wetting was allowed to trickle and flow, forming the eroded rivulets often seen on the sides of railroad earthworks: sort of doing what comes naturally.

6-15 After the soil and rivulets had been formed in the fill, grass was applied and wetted in the same way so that the grass would not clog the natural rivulets. Note mud deposits below.

(fig. 6-7). Tap it gently with a spoon held in the other hand, or shake it by tapping down on the handle with your index finger. This will spread a very light coat of colored dust onto all level surfaces to represent earth. A little will also cling to the irregularities of the cliffs. If the plaster is still so wet that its dust turns to mud, leave it muddy if in a hollow, but add more earth dust to get a loose soil effect in upper regions, slopes, and meadows.

● **Erosion.** Before the earth coat has a chance to fix itself hard, take the syringe, sprayer, or spoon, and dribble water into high-level hollows (fig. 6-12). Use enough water that it flows all the way down to a bucket placed on the floor wherever it must be to catch the overflow. As it runs down, the water will automatically determine a natural watercourse. As in nature, it will wash away soil to bedrock. It will also deposit soil as silt or mud in a natural way in hollows and pools along the way.

While this is another automatic effect, you may find that you have washed away too much soil at the uppermost part of the stream. Redust a little earth here, and use a smaller stream of water.

Do this in all upper-level hollows. Use greater amounts of water in the bigger stream beds. Incidentally, your children will enjoy this step!

● **Grass.** I get good grass effects two ways: one, by using one of the powders listed in the formulas; the other, with flock. The methods are mostly the same, so I'll tell only about the powder method in detail.

First, consider real grass and model railroad grass. They are often miles apart in more ways than one. Until a good coat of house dust settles on it, much model railroad grass is most unrealistic. I learned why when I brought samples of real grass indoors

and matched them to squares of color in a color dictionary. Most real grass is not green as we think of it. It is much closer to the color of the Jeep of World War II — drab, dull, fairly dark, olive-toned. If it is light, it is more yellow than green.

While you may not get the exact Merion blue (matched to my lawn) I get with the formula listed on page 59, because pigments of finer or coarser grind affect the result, I think you will get close to a suitable color. You'll be pleased how this dull-looking color snaps to life when you apply it to the scenery surface.

Don't use more green unless you have to. However, I find I can add a lot of yellow to a mixture without spoiling it, and a yellower mixture is better in dry places or where the soil offers little nourishment. A deeper green grass grows where there is moisture, fertilizer, and usually on north slopes (south slopes south of the Equator).

Use a coarse sieve for most grass applications. Dust the grass over the same places where the soil has already adhered. The dusting should not be so thick as to hide the soil, unless it is in a place representing a moist area.

For rougher effects you can shake sawdust, pencil shavings, and small bits of lichen in some grass powder to color and simulate small plants, coarser grass, and weeds. A very fine mist of water sprayed over them will help fix the powder to the sawdust, or whatever you used, onto the stems and tips without washing it away.

If the grass powder doesn't adhere well even after a little rewetting (in case the surfaces dried before the binding plaster had attached itself), a spray coat of Dullcote or gum arabic water will help hold it in place. If you want a wet sheen to the grass, use Gloss Kote.

● **More washouts.** Grass, in particular, should not be found where soil wouldn't stay put, so another treatment with the syringe is called for to wash away grass that has lodged into bedrock. The syringe will also remove excess grass if you got too much somewhere, if you didn't let it set hard.

You may repeat soil, grass, eroding — even some more plaster finish coating — anytime you think it will improve the overall effect.

● **Flock for grass.** I began to add a little green flock over my finished grass to get the fine effect I first saw on the Emeryville (Calif.) East Bay club layout. I began to mix a little flock into the plaster. Then my son Paul used more flock. Finally I found I could make good grass entirely with flock.

Now I use both flock and grass powder for different effects. Flock grass, or flock drifted into the air to deposit on existing grass, is especially lifelike when backlighted.

For an all-flock mix, the problem is to kill the bright green of the flock. Plaster dust tends *not* to coat the flock fibers. I found a solution in shaking equals parts of green, brown, and yellow flock in a jar. The result looks horrible until you have applied it over a gum-wetted or varnish-sprayed surface, then have killed the natural sheen with Dullcote, Walther's Decal Duller Varnish, or regular varnish.

Flock seems to be most effective representing deep grass in pastures and near streams. Another good pasture effect is created by using powder grass in three sucessive coats, allowing at least 30 minutes between them. Use a coarse sieve. The field tends to get lumpy, typical of some pastures.

● **Dandelions.** This is verging into the detailing field, but the effect is so fine and so easily created that I must suggest it.

There seems to be no limit to the possibilities of using trees in scenery. However, if you intend to build your own trees, there are some things that should be recalled before starting out.

John Allen contends that it is impossible and impractical to attempt to build an absolutely accurate scale model of a tree, and I agree with him 100 percent. This may sound strange coming from John, who has turned out such breathtaking scenery that it sometimes takes an expert to tell the difference between a photo of his pike and a picture of the real thing.

The expert scenerybuilder is like a fine artist creating a realistic painting. Many paintings appear almost photographic in detail when viewed from a distance of a few feet. Yet a close inspection of the canvas will reveal that the artist has not gone to great lengths to paint-in every tiny line of detail. Instead, he combines masses of color together with shading and highlights, giving an illusion of detail.

Cellulose sponges, steel wool, rubber sponges, and ordinary natural sponges from the sea all can be worked into shapes to resemble foliage on trees and shrubs. However, when it comes to the use of steel wool, I would as soon have a nest of irritated cobras in the middle of my railroad room as a steel-wool tree. Not that it can't be made to look good; it can. But the fine steel mesh that goes to make up a ball of steel wool has a habit of dropping off; and I'm afraid it would find its way into some of my permag motors.

BY far the most popular method of making miniature trees, and I think the most realistic (aside from evergreens), is lichen glued onto a trunk that is either a natural shrub clipping or a trunk artificially made from twisted stranded wire.

Lichen (pronounced *like-en*) is a mosslike vegetation that is grayish white in its natural state. Easiest for the hobbyist to obtain is the Norwegian variety, which is imported to this country by florists and hobby supply firms. There are also several useful domestic varieties of lichen which can be found in considerable quantity in Michigan, Georgia, and Florida; however, most American varieties are coarser than imported strains of lichen.

Lichen — treated, dyed, and packaged — can be obtained at most well-stocked hobby shops in a variety of colors. However, if a railroader intends to use lichen in massive lots, this can run into some big money. For large amounts I recommend that you buy the lichen in its raw state. It can be purchased much more economically in this manner and can be treated and dyed in your own home to look just

K. Phillips Kallman.

7-2 Closeup of sandbar of fig. 1-9, page 6. Reeds are pieces of broomstraws; birds, made from modeling clay, have paper wings. Sandbars occur at side of river away from main channel, usually beyond a point of rocks or at the inside of a turn in the stream.

7-3, above: Twig-and-lichen trees set off this trestle on Boyce Martin's HO pike in Kentucky. 7-4, below: Tall timber on Jack Work's railroad is made of dowel tapered by sanding. Note how scenic terrain drops behind to hide its joint with painted backdrop.

as good and to get the same results as the kind of lichen that can be purchased by model railroaders at their neighborhood hobby shops.

Bulk lichen, which is often sold by the bale, has characteristics that require special handling and treatment. In its raw state in the bale, the lichen is compressed, hard, gray, and very brittle. It must be treated or pickled so that it will be in a soft, pliable state before it is used. There are two ways of treating it.

Regardless of which method of treating you use, the lichen should be washed before it is dipped into the pickling solution. To wash it, dump the bale into a large dishpan full of warm water. Let the dry, brittle lichen soak up the warm water. It's like a sponge — the instant it hits the water, it starts fluffing up, absorbing the moisture and softening. After it has soaked a few minutes, start kneading it and picking out the trash, such as pine needles and bits of bark, that may be embedded in it. Remove it from the water, squeezing out all the surplus water at it is lifted from the pan. Now it is ready to be pickled. As mentioned before, there are two ways of doing this.

The first method is to soak it in a solution of 2 parts water to 1 part glycerin. If a great quantity of lichen is to be processed (two bales or more), it will be more economical to use commercial glycerin rather than the chemically pure glycerin which is purchased at the drugstore prescription counter.

To start with, the solution of glycerin and water should be about 200 degrees — not quite at the boiling point. There are several schools of thought as to how long the lichen should remain in this solution. Some say 30 to 40 minutes is long enough; others advocate leaving it immersed in the solution overnight. Personally, I prefer the longer bath.

Andrew Uveges.

7-5 Parts of stems and natural joints of many plants make good tree frames. Bob Barbour of Englewood, N. J., often spent the summer in Colorado, where he picked sagebrush stems for tree frames. If lichen is added, trees look as in fig. 7-1.

Remove the lichen from the glycerin solution; squeeze it as you do, and lay it out on a thick pad of old newspapers to dry for about half an hour. Now it is ready for coloring. Before coloring, let's take a look at the second method of pickling, which is advocated by Bartlett Frost. The procedure begins the same way, by washing first, but the pickling solution is different. Frost makes his pickling solution from 1 part glycerin, 1 part acetone (or lacquer-thinner), and 2 parts alcohol. *Obviously, don't heat this mixture.* Frost contends that the alcohol and acetone in the solution drive the water from the cells of the lichen and it is replaced by the glycerin, which is a heavy, nonevaporating liquid. Frost also recommends leaving the lichen in this pickling solution overnight. After it is removed from the solution, it should be allowed to dry completely before it is colored.

As in pickling, there are several methods of coloring. One way is to dip lichen into a solution made of water and fabric dyes such as Rit, Tintex, or the Putnam dyes. I always add a bit of glycerin to my dye solution. (I prefer the fabric dyes.) You can also add dye to the pickling solution, accomplishing two steps of the process in one. You will of course then need a pickling solution of each color needed. There will always be some pickling solution left over, and it can be stored in fruit jars and used again. However, it should be noted that although the pickling solution can be used again, the glycerin has to be replaced as it is absorbed into the lichen. If a large batch of lichen is processed, glycerin may have to be replaced regularly during the processing. If not replenished, the processed lichen will become dry and brittle after it is removed from the solution and dried.

Another method of coloring the lichen is by use of aniline dye, which is soluble in alcohol. The third method of coloring is to use artist's oil colors mixed in a thin turpentine wash. Make sure this mixture is very thin if the lichen is dipped into it. After the lichen is colored by dipping in any of

Clint Grant.

7-6 Hedge clippings also make tree frames. From left to right are privet; crepe myrtle, two samples; nandina, two samples; and decayed pine cones. Every locality has some weeds and shrubs that can be used for similar tree skeletons. Whole tree frames can be dipped in latex to preserve their shape and sometimes their color.

Clint Grant.

7-7 The same hedge clippings from fig. 7-6 look like this when trimmed with lichen "foliage." The twig limbs are covered with cement and lichen wads are pushed on endwise. To change the appearance of some trees, so all don't resemble lichen, dip some in dull varnish, and dust with green sawdust or flock.

these solutions, the procedure is the same — spread it out on a blanket of old newspapers and let it dry at least 24 hours.

In coloring your lichen, make up several different shades of green, ranging from a light yellow green through a deeper green to an olive green. The reason for this is simple. Take a look at the nearest clump of woods which contains more than one variety of tree. Note that one variety of tree may be a very light green, while another type next to it is of an entirely different shade of green. One should avoid monotony in foliage shape and color just as one avoids it in terrain.

Wɪᴛʜ the lichen prepared and colored, you are ready to form miniature trees. Some prefer to make their own trunks by twisting pieces of stranded wire together: stranded iron clothesline wire, picture-hanging wire, or florist's wire. The number of pieces of wire to be used will vary with the size of the tree and the trunk desired. The pieces of stranded wire are twisted together to form the lower part of the trunk (as shown in fig. 7-8), then divided to form the heavier limbs, and divided again to form the branches. The main part of the trunk can be covered with plaster or wrapped with masking tape to simulate bark, then painted a dark brown.

Coat the strands that form the tree branches either with cement or some adhesive like Elmer's Glue-All. Thread these into the mesh of the green lichen which represents a closely packed mass of leaves. Trees made in this manner can range from a scale 10 or 15 feet, representing young saplings, to a full 60 feet, representing a full-grown tree.

However, making tree trunks from twisted wire always seemed to me like

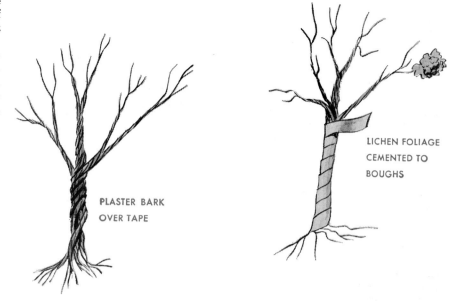

PLASTER BARK OVER TAPE

LICHEN FOLIAGE CEMENTED TO BOUGHS

7-8 Stranded wires are twisted together to make armature for wire tree frame, left. Then masking tape is wound around the wire frame. This can be painted as is, or it can be coated with plaster or brown sawdust.

doing it the hard way, for there are so many twigs that can be clipped from natural shrubs and weeds that more closely resemble a miniature tree. Nature has a peculiar way of duplicating herself in miniature. If you will cast your observant eye around hedges and shrubs and other natural growth, you will be amazed to find tiny branches and twigs that are in reality miniature tree trunks with a branch system.

Certain varieties of sagebrush, which grows wild in such states as New Mexico, Colorado, Texas, and Nevada, have a branch system that makes a perfect tree when trimmed to size. Examples of these sagebrush tree trunks from Bob Barbour's former HO railroad in Englewood, N. J., are shown in figs. 4-4 and 7-1.

Privet hedge, which grows in a temperate climate, is an excellent source of supply for model-size tree trunks — especially if the hedge has been clipped often. Frequent clipping causes new branches to form on the cut ends of the older branches, forming perfect little tree-trunk systems. Another source of supply that is more or less confined to the warmer climates is clippings from nandina and crape myrtle bushes. Branches of the nandina shrubs usually terminate in a cluster of little balls which turn red and eventually fall off in autumn, leaving a perfect little tree skeleton. The same is true of crape myrtle bushes except that the branches are tipped with seed pods in the autumn. These can be pinched off, leaving a miniature tree. Colored lichen can then be cemented to the ends of the branches.

While, as Allen says, it is impracti-

cal to attempt to scale-model any particular species of tree, it is possible, by observing the shapes of trees, to give the impression that your miniature creation is a white oak, an American elm, a maple, an ash, or a linden tree. Shown in figs. 7-10 and 7-11 are typical shapes and their names.

Trees can be "planted" in the terrain by drilling a hole in the plaster the same size as the trunks; this assures a tight, press-fit. Make sure you don't drill the hole too large. Holes too large will allow the trees to flop and droop unrealistically.

Some modelers prefer to fix their trees in place permanently with cement and to model an exposed root system around their bases in plaster or wax. I prefer to have mine removable so that they can be taken out if they are in the way of maintenance work.

There are certain rules, illustrated in fig. 7-12, that should be observed in the planting of trees. Unless you are modeling a fruit orchard, never plant your trees evenly spaced in a straight line or other geometric pattern. Also, it's a good idea to mix-in several sizes, shapes, and types when modeling a clump of trees growing wild on the mountainside.

It also adds realism to the scene to mingle a few evergreens, such as cedars and small firs, along with the leaf-bearing trees. And, if you are modeling a wild, unkempt part of country, there are always a few old dead trees lifting their naked limbs among the foliage of the leaf bearers. These are the trees that have been struck by lightning, killed by insects, or have died from some other cause.

7-9 Cemented sagebrush twigs ready for wads of lichen. Parts of twigs can be broken off or other parts can be added for any shaping effect. These are twigs of sagebrush from western Colorado, trimmed short near the joints.

OBLONG	CONICAL	COLUMNAR
(WHITE PINE)	(HEMLOCK)	(RED CEDAR)

7-10 Evergreen tree shapes.

ROUND	OBLONG	LONG OBLONG	COLUMNAR	VASE-SHAPED
(MAPLE — ASH — LINDEN)	(HONEY LOCUST — COTTONWOOD)	(WHITE OAK)	(LOMBARDY POPLAR)	(AMERICAN ELM)

7-11 Deciduous tree shapes, summer foliage.

In a well-kept park area they are chopped down immediately, but out in the countryside no one seems to care whether they fall or stand.

If you are using ready-made trees, don't plant a forest of all the same-size trees. Mix-in a few smaller trees and shrubs for variety. Also discard trees that droop and flop over at unnatural angles. In planting a clump of trees, remember that the taller trees are usually found in the middle, while the smaller ones that bear the brunt of the winds and elements are usually found around the perimeter of the woods or forest. Trees at the edge of the woods or in the open have many side branches, while trees in mid-forest have few branches except up near the top where light is plentiful.

Before moving on to other construction methods, there's one neat little trick that can be done with lichen which I'd like to pass on to you. Lichen can be used in massive proportions to give the impression of a heavily wooded forest without going to the trouble of making each individual tree in the grove of trees. Fig. 7-13 explains this method at a glance. I believe it was introduced to the hobby by the late Frank Ellison.

Select the area to be heavily wooded. Then, by means of wooden blocks, or pegs made from ¼" or ½" dowel, support a netting of small-mesh chicken wire or ½"-mesh hardware cloth roughly the shape of the desired "forest" about 2" or 3" (larger in O gauge) above the plaster hillside. To this mesh attach large clumps of lichen of various shades of green. This represents the *tops* of the trees in the center of the forest. Hairpin-shaped soft iron wire threaded down through the lichen into the mesh of the hardware cloth can be used to fix the lichen treetops in place. Twist the ends of the hairpin wire together *underneath* the hardware cloth. Make sure that the lichen is applied so thick that it is impossible to see the hardware cloth or the wire hairpins holding it in place.

BAD

SPOTTY, POORLY SPACED TREES

GOOD

GRADUAL FOLIAGE BUILDUP FROM SMALL TO LARGE TREES WITH SMALL SHRUBS DOTTED ABOUT BASES

AVOID DROOPY TREES — CAUSED BY LOOSE FIT IN PLASTER OR TOO-LIMBER TRUNK

TREES ERECT — MANY BRANCHES — REALISTICALLY SPACED BOUGHS

AVOID TREES SAME SIZE, COLOR AND SHAPE (SUCH AS DIMESTORE CHRISTMAS TREES) IN AN ABSOLUTELY STRAIGHT LINE

7-12

EVERGREENS OF DIFFERENT TYPES AND HEIGHTS MINGLED WITH LEAF-BEARING TREES — THROW IN AN OCCASIONAL DEAD OR DYING TREE

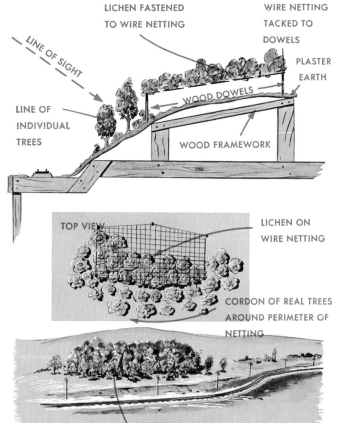

LICHEN FASTENED TO WIRE NETTING

WIRE NETTING TACKED TO DOWELS

PLASTER EARTH

LINE OF SIGHT

LINE OF INDIVIDUAL TREES

WOOD DOWELS

WOOD FRAMEWORK

TOP VIEW

LICHEN ON WIRE NETTING

CORDON OF REAL TREES AROUND PERIMETER OF NETTING

FINISHED APPEARANCE FROM VIEWING ANGLE GIVES IMPRESSION OF **MANY** INDIVIDUAL TREES

7-13 Simulating a forest.

Around this trunkless treetop forest, plant a row or two of individual trees, complete with trunks and their branch systems. Some shrubs of various types on the ground will help hide the fact that the treetops in the middle have no trunks. The result is a wooded area that looks as if it contained hundreds of individual trees. This time it's a case of not being able to see the trees for the forest.

SOME of the most realistic trees I've ever seen on a model railroad are those towering evergreens made by John Allen and Jack Work. Both use the same method of construction. They use tapered wood dowels to represent the trunks, and cement pimosa asparagus fern into holes drilled in the trunks to form the boughs. I once asked John just what type of tree these miniatures were supposed to represent. He told me that they were not intended to be a scale model of any particular type, but were supposed to give the illusion of some of the tall evergreens that grow in various parts of the country, more especially the West.

I've made quite a number of these trees for my own layout, and it is interesting to note the reaction of visitors to them. One fellow will call them "pines," the next visitor will refer to them as "firs," and the next guy to trudge up my attic stairs will dub them "redwoods" or "cedars."

Fig. 7-14 shows the modeling method. These trees may range to 130 scale feet in height. Jack Work points out that there have been recorded instances of these western evergreens having a trunk *diameter* of 15 actual feet and towering several hundred feet in height. However, he adds that we should use a little caution in attempting to model trees so large, or we will tend to dwarf our mountains by trees relatively too tall for them. Jack says that in the average room, with 8-foot ceiling, it is possible to build a mountain only about 700 scale feet high, even if we start at the floor. So such things as trees and other objects in the scene should be kept in reasonable proportion if we wish to give the impression that the mountain towers thousands of feet.

If you intend to use balsa to form the trunks for these trees, make sure you get *hard* balsa. Balsa comes in two grades, you know — soft and hard. The soft balsa tends to break when tapered to a sharp point, and even the hard balsa must be handled with extreme care. Balsa stripwood, either ¾₁₆" x ¾₁₆" or ¼" x ¼", is about the right size to use. It is sold at hobby shops in 3-foot lengths at a few cents per strip. I usually make three tree trunks out of each length. By the time I've

allowed for an inch to "plant" in my plaster, I have what amounts to an evergreen about 80 scale feet high.

Another material source is cedar shingles. They have a natural taper; if sawed in strips to equal their thickness at the base, you have excellent raw material for the trunks.

The square stripwood can be tapered by holding the wood in one hand and rotating it against a coarse file in your other hand, or by twisting it in a bit of coarse garnet paper held between the fingers. It is also possible to chuck the larger or base end of the trunk in a power drill or lathe and apply the taper with a file or sandpaper. Some time can be saved by carefully whittling the wood to a taper with a knife, then smoothing and finishing it with abrasive paper or with a file.

After the trunk is formed, it should be stained a dark grayish brown. I use old lacquer thinner in which I've been cleaning brushes. Usually the mixture of locomotive black, silver, and tuscan red gives me exactly the shade I want to have on my trees.

When the tapered dowel trunk is smoothed and stained, it is ready for the branches and boughs. Using a small drill, about a no. 70 held in a pin vise, drill holes at staggered intervals in the trunk. These are for the insertion of the fern boughs. Drill two holes through the trunk at 90-degree angles to permit the insertion of a group of four branches at each location. The spacing between branch groupings should become progressively closer from bottom to top. However, in modeling some of the older trees which have started to lose their foliage, it is a good idea to skip irregular distances, leaving the trunk bare.

Jack Work prefers to drill all holes before starting to attach the branches, but I like to drill mine as I go along, drilling one set of holes, cementing the butt end of the branches to the trunk, then moving up the trunk to

7-15 Jack Work adds asparagus fern to holes in dowel tree trunk. See fig. 8-1.

the next grouping and drilling again. Near the top of the tree, where the taper becomes almost as fine as the drill, it is impossible to put holes through the trunk. At this point, the branches are cemented directly to it.

It may take a little hunting to locate a source of the proper type of fern to use on these trees. It is grown chiefly in Florida and can be found at florists' shops and some hobby stores, and in some cases at the same counter with flowercraft supplies at either Woolworth or Kresge stores. It is a lacy, delicate growth used in making floral arrangements. If you get it in the untreated state from a florist, pickle it in the same manner as lichen, using the warm-water, glycerin-dye bath.

In asking for the fern, use the full name, pimosa asparagus fern, for I've discovered that in some parts it is referred to merely as "pimosa," while other dealers call it "asparagus fern." The last time I bought some I asked for "pimosa asparagus" and was told by the saleslady, "We don't have any of that but we do have asparagus pimosa." An examination proved it to be what I had bought at another branch of the same store under the name of "pimosa fern."

If you happen to be fortunate enough to live in a section of the country where fern or various types of moss grow wild, you will not be so dependent upon commercial firms for your supply of foliage. You can gather your

SQUARE BALSA
¾₁₆" x ¾₁₆"
OR ¼" x ¼"

ASPARAGUS FERN LEAF
CEMENTED INTO HOLES

9" to 12"

TAPER BALSA TO POINTED DOWEL

TAPERED

FOR PLANTING

TRUNK CUT
FROM CEDAR
SHINGLE

FOR HEAVIER LIMBS
SHRUB TWIGS CAN BE
CEMENTED IN HOLES

7-14 **Dowel tree construction.**

7-16 Some leaves have fallen from the trees on this Detroit museum scene. Seeing through branches displays more of the modelwork. Note retaining wall below tracks.

George Kawamoto.

own foliage on field trips, bring it home, and treat it. Some of Work's most realistic evergreens are made from a type of mossy fern which he gathers in his neck of the woods in the Pacific Northwest. These field trips, either conducted as a special project or as a sideline to a family picnic jaunt or a vacation, can be gold mines when it comes to gathering material for foliage and trees on the model railroad.

An author often lists construction materials and supply sources for his readers. But, Work points out, in the case of the search for natural foliage, this is quite useless for a number of reasons. First and most important, mosses, ferns, and weeds that are perfect miniature foliage may grow in profusion in one section of the country but not even exist in other sections. Second, they may be known in one area under one name, and in a section a few hundred miles away be known by some other name.

Identifying foliage by Latin names would be meaningless to all except students of botany, and it's safe to say that the botanists are a minority among model railroaders. On the other hand, it often happens that a variety of shrub that produces a passable miniature tree in its foliage in one part of the country grows in a slightly different shape or size, making it unsuitable for model use, in another state. An example of this is sumac, sometimes spelled sumach or shumac, a shrub bearing small conical clusters of red berries. It is found in most sections of the country; in some parts it forms such perfect little miniature trees that

it has been clipped, dyed, treated, and sold commercially in hobby shops as scale model trees. However, the variety of sumac found near my home in Texas grows in such a gnarled and twisted shape, and its berries are so large (everything's BIG in Texas), that it's not very suitable for model trees.

The thing to do on field trips is to make the best of what is at hand. Train yourself to see and think in terms of scale size and texture. It is easy to discount weeds and foliage as "out of scale" when actually their sizes in relation to surrounding growths cause them to lose all meaning and proportion. So says Work in urging modelers to make field trips in search of miniature vegetation. For instance, a weed or shrub that looks entirely too large for model use growing in its natural state may produce a perfect tree trunk with limb and branch system if properly trimmed with clippers.

MANY weeds and plants wilt quickly and must be treated or preserved if they are to be used in modelwork. The glycerin and water treatment tends to keep any sort of vegetation soft. In some cases, this is not desirable. For instance, on one of my many vacation trips to nearby Colorado I discovered an unidentified weed (a bush of the spirea family) which makes a perfect HO scale lombardy poplar tree. The trouble was, this weed dried out quickly, and in its dry state tended to lose its foliage and seed pods which combined to give it a tree shape. By experimenting, I found that by dipping the freshly clipped weed heads in shellac it was

possible to preserve them indefinitely. The shellac covering served as an adhesive that stiffened the entire branch system and held the foliage in place. After the shellac treatment, the weeds were spray-painted flat green.

Other inexhaustible sources of miniature trees that I discovered in Colorado were the partially rotted cones found under the huge evergreens — firs and pines. Freshly fallen pine and fir cones look exactly like what they are, fallen cones, so are unsuitable. But after they have lain on the ground for some time and have been subjected to the action of sun, wind, rain, snow, and ice, the flaky covering of the cones starts to rot and fall away, leaving a tiny maze of tough fibers that reach upward in a conical shape. Spray-painted a dark green color, they bear a striking resemblance to a small cedar, arbor vitae, or a seedling pine tree. Examples of these miniature evergreens can be seen in fig. 7-6.

For those wishing to make the taller evergreens but who find it difficult to locate a supply of pimosa or asparagus fern, there are other growths which make excellent foliage for the balsa trunks. While searching Woolworth's flowercraft counter in search of materials I ran across a bundle of air fern. Apparently this fern is already treated — or else it needs no treatment, taking its nourishment from the air — for it remains green indefinitely. When applied to the tapered balsa trunks, it bears a good resemblance to a ponderosa pine.

Another source of evergreen foliage is yarrow. Both Bartlett Frost and M. B. Wakefield have achieved realistic results using yarrow both as the branches of a scraggly old pine and as a variety of deciduous tree. Yarrow is a common weed found in most states. It grows in empty lots, along roadsides, and in ungrazed fields. The flower has a flat, horizontal top made up of numerous fine blossoms held up by an intricate twig system that branches out at angles. When these twigs are separated, the blossoms dyed a dark green and inserted in a tapered balsa trunk, they bear a resemblance to bunches of pine needles. See figs. 7-17 and 7-18.

Yarrow is ideal for O and S scale, fair for HO, but a trifle oversize for TT and N scales. It is found in its best growth in late autumn or early winter. It also can be found in florist shops, as it is often used as a prop in making flower arrangements. This same yarrow can be used in making other varieties of trees, including the leafed types. A complete "head" of yarrow makes an excellent dwarf tree or shrub.

8-1 Finished scene on Jack Work's railroad. See fig. 7-14 for tree construction and several photos in chapter 4 (fig. 4-29) for the construction of this entire scene. Note how some trees have curved trunks and stubs where lower branches have "dropped off."

is unrealistic — even if you could find one of the right color.

Now, let's look at the various advantages of these methods and see if they outweigh the disadvantages.

Liquid casting plastic is one of the most realistic methods of all of creating artificial water, for if applied in sufficient thickness, it gives depth. It looks wet, and it is possible, by careful modeling, to capture in still life the flow of the stream as it swirls past rocks in the riverbed. Cost could be a bit high if the area to be covered is large.

Linn Westcott has found that flexible silicone rubbers, used in potting electronic circuits (including the old Astrac receivers), is a very fine medium. It has all the good qualities of liquid casting plastic and is made with two parts mixed together in the same way. But when it sets it becomes rubber, as clear as water, rather than

rigid. You can cut it later to make repairs, then put the plug back in invisibly or else pour in new material. Shrinkage is no problem, and it would also be possible to make moving waves by mechanical or pneumatic means. The material is very expensive, so is suited more for brooks than for rivers or lakes. Several grades are made, differing in setting time. Linn has used General Electric RTV-602 "Clear Silicone Potting Compound," which is made by GE's Silicone Products Department at Waterford, New York. This sets overnight.

One of the problems of these two materials has not yet been solved. This is their tendency to creep up the sides of their river or lake basins. A little plaster coating may have to be brought down over this meniscus edge to hide it.

Polymer varnishes, also ordinary latex, have possibilities also worth ex-

ploring in this kind of work, Linn suggests.

Dust accumulating over any of these chemical "waters" can be washed away with water and a soft brush.

Cyanite or ripple glass gives the appearance of depth and a certain sense of motion to the water. It can be colored in graduating tones. Because it is semitransparent, it is possible to look down through it and see the river or lake bottom. Its cost is comparatively low.

Shellacked plaster is probably the lowest in cost and the fastest and easiest method of simulating water. While it may not have the advantage of transparency, it has the advantage that waves can be modeled. (Because they simulate frozen motion, they look better to the camera than to the eye.) A fine example is in fig. 8-2.

Waterglass, like plastic, gives the appearance of depth.

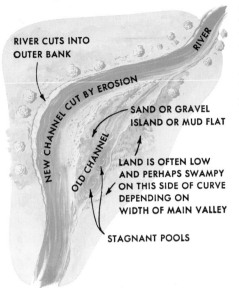

RIVER CUTS INTO OUTER BANK

RIVER

NEW CHANNEL CUT BY EROSION

OLD CHANNEL

SAND OR GRAVEL ISLAND OR MUD FLAT

LAND IS OFTEN LOW AND PERHAPS SWAMPY ON THIS SIDE OF CURVE DEPENDING ON WIDTH OF MAIN VALLEY

STAGNANT POOLS

8-3 Rivers always cut banks at outside of curve, leave deposits at inner side.

Sheet plywood rippled with plastic wood has the same advantages as shellacked plaster in that it is cheap and easy to construct. The cost is slightly higher than the plaster, but not as expensive as the ripple glass or liquid casting plastic methods.

Real water has the advantage of actual movement — it can be made to flow and it is possible to actually move boats over its surface or to make mill wheels turn.

About the only advantage to the blue mirror method is its ease of installation.

BEFORE delving into the technicalities of model lake and river construction, let's briefly review a few of the characteristics of real water so we'll know what the problems are.

A river or creek is a mass of water on the move down a definite groove or channel in the earth, dropping from higher to lower ground. Speed of the movement of water depends upon the angle at which it descends. Mountain streams that drop rapidly down steep slopes will flow faster than the more sluggish streams that course through flatter country. For a navigable river, the slope is small; it may drop only 10 inches in a mile of flow.

Flowing water causes both lateral and vertical erosion; for this reason, the appearance of a river may gradually change. In the case of a river that twists and bends, this erosion is always greatest at the outer bank of the turns and at the foot of rapids. Water flows more slowly around the inner bank of the curve and beyond the pool below a rapids, leaving deposits of silt. Since the outer bank is being cut away at a more rapid rate, mostly during floods, it will be steeper, while the inner bank, subject to siltation, may actually build up and become a gentle slope.

In the case of a reverse or S bend in the river, erosion may eventually cut through the center curve or bend, forming a new channel and leaving a small island between the new and old channels. A small pool may be left in the old channel, fed by overflow from the new channel when it rains. (See fig. 8-3.) Very similar erosion occurs in streams that flow through solid rock mountains, just as it does where the stream races through muddy or sandy country. However, it may take centuries for deep erosion to occur in the rocks, whereas sharp erosion in clay or mud banks is just a matter of a few years — even months if the rainfall is above average.

Freshwater lakes come under two general classifications: natural and man-made. Natural lakes occur where the flow or drainage of water is trapped by a deep depression in the earth caused by warpage of the earth's surface, or erosion by a glacier in the ice age. Landslips or river debris also can stop the natural flow of water and create a natural lake.

Artificial lakes are made by man throwing an earthen or concrete dam across the channel of a river or creek. Types of dams vary according to surrounding terrain. In rugged western mountains these dams are massive, nearly vertical concrete walls extending across a canyon from the face of one rocky cliff to another. In flatter lands the dam may be all earthwork with a protecting layer of rock riprap on the water side to prevent erosion from waves. Dams constructed in the flatter plains country for the purpose of flood control, or for power use, usually are a combination of the two methods. The earth fill may be used for the greater part of the dam, but usually in the center there is a concrete section where the flood gates are located.

Somewhere in between the natural and artificial lakes are those created by the beavers. These little animals, in building their homes, often dam mountain or woodland streams, creating lakes. They certainly couldn't be called man-made, yet they are not due to any natural erosion or faults in the earth. Let's just call 'em eagerbeaver dams and let it go at that.

The color of water is governed largely by the terrain through which it flows. Pure water is crystal-clear, but as it flows it takes on the color of the land through which it travels. A stream from melted snow flowing through a rocky bed in the mountains, which produces little if any sediment to discolor the water, will be crystalclear. A river flowing over a heavily silted bed will stir up some of the deposits and may be a reddish orange or various shades of brown ranging from a clayish yellow to a muddy brown.

Unless it is under unusual conditions, such as a raging flood which stirs up the riverbed sediment, all normal flowing water in a river takes on a varying color as it becomes deeper. Shallow water is fairly clear; thus it takes on the color of the bed showing through along its edges. As the water gets deeper it changes to green, then to blue-green, then to blue; in the case of very deep water, it is almost a deep purple-black. The clearer the water, the deeper these hues — depending upon the natural overhead light and angle of the sun.

The angle you view water from also makes a difference. From an airplane or high bridge, water is rarely blue at all unless extremely deep. But from a low angle the water acts almost like a perfect mirror and reflects the sky or distant trees and shows little of its own color. A good surface on modeled water can also reflect sky backdrops or distant rocks or trees.

BEFORE launching into a description of the various methods of waterway construction, there is one more

8-4 Construction of lakes and rivers can be done by following the same methods, but the rivers must disappear behind hills or other scenic barriers to obtain the best illusion of continuation.

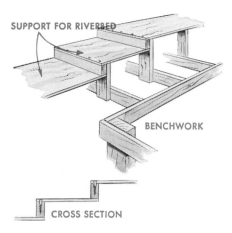

8-5 **Descending base for plastic river allows for cataracts over hard rock strata.**

angle I'd like to stress. The step-by-step mechanics of construction *are the same* for either a lake, a pond, a creek, or a river, *as long as the method is the same!*

To clarify this, maybe it would be better to say that if you have decided upon using the plastic method of building your waterways, you will use the same step-by-step procedure in creating a lake as you do in constructing a river. The one difference is that in construction of a lake, the water is level and the banks encircle the complete body of water. But in creating a river there should be a very, very slight incline to make the flow of water logical — and the river and its banks should seem to continue indefinitely. They may run off any edge of the tablework; or if you don't care for this treatment the river may wander out of sight back of a hill or clump of trees, as shown in fig. 8-4. One end could be treated one way and the other end the other way.

To avoid needless repetition as I go from method to method in my description of construction procedure, I will describe only one type of waterway for each method. But the reader will

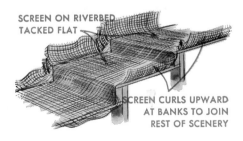

SCREEN ON RIVERBED
TACKED FLAT

SCREEN CURLS UPWARD
AT BANKS TO JOIN
REST OF SCENERY

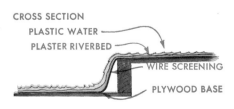

CROSS SECTION
PLASTIC WATER
PLASTER RIVERBED
WIRE SCREENING
PLYWOOD BASE

8-6 **Screen wire is tacked to river base.**

bear in mind that each method described can be used for the construction of any type of waterway.

To look like real water our model lakes and rivers must *appear* to have depth. What gives artificial water the appearance of depth? The answer is: a graded transparency that enables the spectator to actually look down through the artificial water and *see* the bottom of the lake or river. That is why the two plastic and the cyanite (ripple glass) methods are so much more realistic than others.

Plastic method

The plastic method was first publicized by west coast railroader W. S. (Bill) Graves in the article "Plastic Lakes and Streams" in the November 1951 issue of MODEL RAILROADER. If you can latch onto a copy of this ancient issue, I suggest that everyone contemplating using the plastic method read it, for Graves goes into much greater detail in his article than space will permit me to do here. However, I will give sufficient information for the average builder to construct a lake or stream.

Let's say you want to construct a rushing mountain stream. The first step is most important, and that is the construction of a sturdy foundation for the rushing river. Whereas screen wire allowed to sag, or papier-mâché on cardboard strips, may be sufficiently strong for the creation of a lake bed using other methods, the plastic type of construction demands a *strong foundation*, fastened into place preferably by flathead wood screws. Plastic, if flowed over a flimsy foundation such as unsupported screen wire, tends to crack with the slightest shifting movement of its base. So, use at least a ¼"-thick sheet of plywood slightly larger than the width and length of the stream. Fasten it to the framework at the desired depth *below track level* and give it a very slight inclination. If waterfalls in the stream are desired, build the plywood foundation on three different levels as shown in a cross-section view in fig. 8-5.

The next step is to tack ordinary window screen flat and securely over the plywood, allowing an excess margin to curl upwards at the edges where you plan the banks of the river, as in fig. 8-6. Hard shell could be used instead. Now what you're going to do is first model the riverbed, then cover it with several thin layers of liquid plastic. This plastic, when it hardens, assumes a semitransparency which simulates the murkiness of water. The plastic is not to be applied in great thicknesses. It is amazing how a few coats of plastic, less than ½" thick, takes on the appearance of a deep, rushing stream.

Keep this in mind in constructing your lake or riverbed and make it only slightly less than the top level the water is to be when completed.

Using the same type of plaster you used to construct your mountains, model the riverbed. Apply the plaster generously enough to entirely hide the mesh if you used wire screening. Apply it with a trowel; then smooth it with a brush. Where the plaster curves upward to become the riverbanks, make it rough and jagged to represent eroded granite and stone. Small mounds of plaster about ⅛" to ³⁄₁₆" high and 2" to 3" long can be formed to represent sandbars or rocks below the water's surface. (These dimensions are suggested for HO.)

If the river is to be extremely fast-flowing, with rapids and a choppy surface, then the plaster riverbed should be rather rough. For instance, a series of mounds ranging in height from ¼" to ½" high — sort of a washboard effect only not so uniform — running crosswise to the flow of the river will simulate rapids when covered with several coats of the plastic material.

Anything which might logically be found embedded in the bed of a flowing stream should be inserted at this time in the wet plaster. Such things as rocks (part of which will stick above the surface of the water), old tree trunks representing driftwood lodged in the bottom, piers, retaining walls, reeds, or what have you, all should be fixed in place at this time.

8-7 **River details.**

Actually, what you are doing in part at this stage of the game is to model to some extent the shape of the flow of the top level of the water in the contour of the bottom of the river. In placing objects such as trees and rocks that are supposed to protrude above the water, keep in mind that the final coat of plastic which covers the plaster riverbed will be at least ³⁄₁₆" thick. After all this modeling in plaster is finished and all rocks are in place, the work should be allowed to dry completely for at least 2 days — possibly longer if there is a lot of humidity in the air.

Next step is the painting of the riverbed and all areas to be covered by the plastic. Actually what you do at this stage is to add some "water tones" of color to the bed itself, for while the plastic material will be dyed or toned to represent various shades of water at different depths, coloring on the bottom also serves as a sort of crutch to support the tinting in the transparent plastic and heighten the illusion of depth.

One of the best references for the proper colors is nature itself. If there is a creek or river near your home, take a look at it. If it's a fairly clear stream, you'll notice that the color of the riverbed shows through near the banks where the water is shallow and goes to a green to blue-green to blue as it becomes deeper near the middle. Of course, if it is a river fed by drainage off cultivated farmlands, it probably will be muddy from bank to bank and there will be little difference in color. Such streams are dull, drab, and uninteresting to model when compared to such colorful streams as the Las Animas, which rages down the rocks of the Animas Canyon between Durango and Silverton, Colorado.

Let's suppose you've decided your river is to be a fairly clear mountain stream. Using either oils or water-base paint, stain the entire riverbed an earth color that logically blends with the color of the surrounding earth and rocks — say a yellowish brown. Using medium chrome green and ultramarine blue, gradually change the color to a deeper hue near the middle of the riverbed and in spots where deep pools might logically be. In all cases, the color changes should be gradual—not spotted like the splotches on a marine's camouflage battle jacket. Dry-brush specks of white over the rough edges of the plaster around rocks or rapids where white water or whitecaps might naturally occur in real, swiftly flowing water.

After this painting job is completed and dried, you are ready to start applying the plastic. That's the stuff that gives your river the appearance of being wet.

Graves, in his MODEL RAILROADER article, advises to start the pouring of the plastic onto the plaster riverbed in the morning, as it can be a time-consuming project. The plastic he used was made by the Kemnitz Corporation of Milwaukee and was called Plaskit 56. There are now many makers of casting resin intended for embedding objects in paperweights and the like. You can also use the plastic intended for making fiberglass boats. This latter sometimes has a yellowish color, but if it is transparent this will not spoil the water effect, as many streams and some lakes have iron in the water. The materials can also be dyed to greenish or bluish tones when desired, using special colors sold for the purpose.

In purchasing the resin, take into consideration that a pint will cover roughly 4 square feet approximately $3/16$″ thick. Some authorities differ on whether it is necessary to use heat to age or set the plastic. In his original instructions, Graves recommends the use of a 150-watt household light bulb in a reflector to throw the heat downward as a means of hardening the plastic. However, in a later issue of the "Blue Book of Model Railroad Practice" in the section devoted to scenery, it is pointed out that the application of heat is not strictly necessary. One word of advice: Don't start this application of plastic on a dusty day — particularly if you happen to live in a section of the Midwest or West subject to periodical sand or dust storms.

A good selection of dyes to tone the the clear plastic would include yellow, green, blue, brown, and white. Tools include a wide-mouthed, clear glass jar (such as a pint-size fruit jar), an old tablespoon for mixing, and a clean paintbrush for spreading the plaster as it is poured on the riverbed.

For the first coat, mix a batch of about 15 to 20 tablespoons of the resin and catalyst combination in the fruit jar. The plastic can be used clear and will give a very realistic result. In my opinion, the resin with a little dye coloring added will be more lifelike and will seem to add motion to the water.

Assuming you've decided to add the dyes, proceed with caution, for some kinds are very intense and should be added sparingly to the clear resin and catalyst mix. Use an eyedropper. Select a dye that approximates the average overtone of the plaster riverbed — a light blue-green. Add a few drops of the green dye at a time to the clear plaster mix. Hold the mix up to the light; and remember, not enough dye is better than too much. If you do put too much dye in the mix, it can be thinned by adding additional clear resin, remembering, of course, to add a proportionate amount of the catalyst. In mixing this first coat, remember at all times that you want this plastic mixture to be transparent when it covers the riverbed, so don't get too intense a shade of dye in it.

When you've arrived at the proper shade, pour it on the riverbed. Cover every surface that is eventually supposed to be underwater. Carefully smooth it to a thickness of about $1/16$″. Let this first coat stand undisturbed and not subject to severe temperature changes for 3 hours. This is known as the jelling period. During this period, the mixture generates heat within itself and thickens and jells. Some brands may take longer.

After the jelling period, the plastic is ready for hardening — or curing, as some call it. A temperature of between 90 and 200 degrees is recommended. Graves recommends the use of a 150-watt bulb in a reflector moved about above the surface of the plastic about 2″ away from it. (Don't let the plastic get so hot, however, that it bubbles or burns.) This hardening process can take as long as 2 more hours. However, the whole process is hastened if the room temperature is between 90 and 100 degrees. (This is a cinch for us Texans.)

The container, spoon, and brush can be cleaned with paint and varnish remover.

When the first layer has become hard, or slightly tacky to the touch, it is time to apply a second coat. It is this second coat which gives the "special effects." Smaller batches of different colors are mixed and applied where appropriate. Put deeper greens and blues over spots where deep pools in the river are located. White, representing foam, streaked and following the motion of the water, should go around waterfalls, rapids, and rocks protruding out of the water. In applying the white, don't make it too even; use a dry-brush technique, pulling the brush along lightly in a wavy motion. Put some spots of brown where pools of stagnant water might have accumulated. Fig. 8-8 shows a waterfall.

Follow the same procedure as used to jell and harden the first coat. Since these "special-effect coats" are not as thick as the first coat of plastic, hardening time may be cut to 1 hour.

To apply the last coat, mix it almost clear, with just a slight tint of the base color of blue-green. The amount of catalyst in this final layer should be

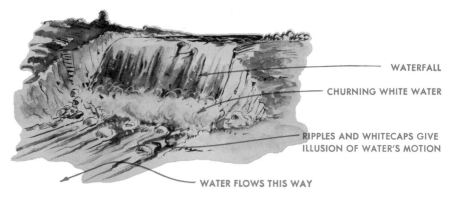

WATERFALL

CHURNING WHITE WATER

RIPPLES AND WHITECAPS GIVE ILLUSION OF WATER'S MOTION

WATER FLOWS THIS WAY

8-8 **Waterfall details.**

Art Schmidt.

8-11 Underwater growth and bottom was made first on "The HO Railroad That Grows"; then glass coated with blue alcohol color and Krylon spray was added. Bottom detail shows through glass. Don't get blue too dark; it reduces light twice, going in and reflecting out, so should be half as dark as you think.

doubled. Doubling the catalyst in the final coat makes it act as a sealer and therefore the final coat is less likely to remain tacky after it is cured.

Now, if you have taken reasonable pains and not rushed things, the result should be a raging mountain stream that looks so wet your visitors will have to reach out and touch it to assure themselves it isn't real water rushing down your plaster canyon.

Silicone rubber method

The method Linn Westcott used with silicone rubber potting compound can also be an alternate method for using the resin already described. A river or lake bed, or harbor, is formed with hard shell (explained in chapter 5) and is detailed with an added coating of plaster as mentioned in chapter 6. The coloring is made much lighter than for surface earth because the plastic greatly darkens it through its "wetting" effect.

Color can be added to the river or lake bed to represent deep water.

8-9 Glass sandwiched between plywood sheets.

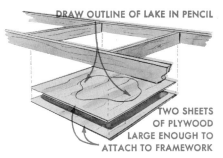

8-10 Glass sandwich is fastened at lake site. Be sure wires never pass below as lake may need repairs and then couldn't be removed as easily.

The silicone rubber already mentioned is then mixed and merely poured into the basin or riverbed. It seeks its own level and if poured at the top of a stream course it will flow slowly downward, filling each pool and finding its way realistically over the rapids areas already modeled. It's a good idea to use two pourings, as the amount for the second can be closely estimated for minimum waste. Any excess is poured into hollows elsewhere on the layout to represent farm ponds, swamps, and the like. No heat is required for curing.

With both this and the resin method, Linn says, it is important to stir in the catalyst making as few bubbles as possible. Usually the bubbles will come to the surface before the material sets, but it is possible to trap the very small bubbles if too many are created.

A neat trick is to put a few simulated fish on top of the surface of the first pouring so they are trapped partway down in the water. Sunken logs, weeds, and other debris also enhance the submerged areas.

Sheet glass method

One of the most satisfactory ways of modeling a small lake or pond is

8-12 Top-mounted sandwich raises water level.

8-13 Bottom-mounted sandwich for steep banks.

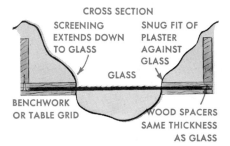

8-14 Pondside banks and bottom.

the cyanite or ripple glass method. Briefly described, this method is merely the sandwiching of a piece of glass between two pieces of plywood. See fig. 8-9.

The top and bottom slabs of plywood are cut out in the center with a jigsaw, in identical contours. The top piece of plywood serves as a foundation for the perimeter of the lake's banks. The bottom plywood serves as a foundation for the lake bottom. The sheet of glass sandwiched in between the two represents the surface of the water. It is possible to look through its semitransparent surface (after it has been lightly tinted) and see the lake bottom. See fig. 8-11.

This popular method of building a model pond or lake has been used by such craftsmen in the hobby as John Allen, the late Frank Ellison, M. B. Wakefield, Larry Kumferman, and others. Each of these has added variations that are sound amendments to the basic formula. The steps in building the lake are simpler and faster

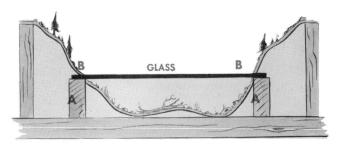

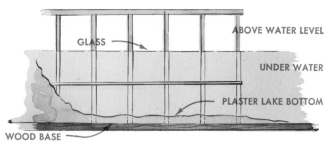

8-15 Showing permanent glass lake. After supports A are in place, the lake bottom is constructed first. Next the glass, stained blue, is put in place resting on supports A. Plaster banks above the water level are the last thing added to lake. Make certain the banks match the contour below water at B.

8-16 Pier or trestle over pond.

than those described in creating the plastic river.

First, select the location for your lake, making sure there is no electrical wiring beneath the area that might interfere with the placement of the lake bottom. Next, select a piece of plywood (I prefer at least ½″ for added strength — but ¼″ will do) large enough to be attached to the open part of the gridwork as shown in fig. 8-10. In pencil, draw the general outline of the lake. Cut the opening for the lake with a saber saw, or a keyhole saw, and you'll have the opening for your lake. Using this upper piece as a pattern, cut an identical opening in the second sheet of plywood.

You have two choices in mounting the top slab of plywood, depending upon how high you want your water level. A low water level results in deeper banks around the pool: compare fig. 8-12 with fig. 8-13. You'll run into less possible trouble mounting the plywood-glass sandwich below your framework joists as in 8-13. If you prefer the higher position, 8-12, be sure you allow ample clearance underneath for raising the glass and lower half of the plywood pair into place.

With the top cutout firmly screwed or nailed in place, permanently, run your screen or other plaster support material down to the BOTTOM edge of the cutout portion as shown in fig. 8-14. Next, tack strips of wood the same thickness as the pane of glass to the underside of the plywood. Put the glass in place and hold it there temporarily by screwing the bottom plywood cutout to the top, as shown in fig. 8-14.

The glass is put in place temporarily to act as a stop for the plasterwork on the lake banks. Model the riverbanks in the same method described earlier, being sure to bring the wet plaster all the way down to the glass. Don't be afraid to let some waste plaster slop over onto the glass. You are striving for a tight fit between the lake banks and the glass-water top. You

want no gaping spaces along the edges of the bank where the earth and rocks join the water.

Let these lake banks dry overnight with the glass in place. This keeps the damp plaster from drooping down below the glass level. After the plaster is dry enough to stay in place, remove the bottom slab of plywood, take out the glass, and wash the plaster smears off it with water. Set the glass aside. Take the bottom plywood cutout to the workbench and build the lake bottom of the material of your choice — screen wire or cardboard strips covered with paper. It can be as deep or as shallow as you wish. This depends largely upon the size of the lake. I'd say even the largest lake (in HO) shouldn't be deeper than 6 (actual) inches. Three to 4 inches at the deepest parts with the lake bed slanting upward at the edge is about right.

Cover the lake bottom with plaster. Embed anything that comes to mind that might logically be found in a lake bed in the wet plaster: old tires, a sunken boat, waterlogged trees, iron drums or tanks. After the plaster bottom has dried, paint it following the same general plan as described for the riverbed: deep blues in the middle at the deepest part, fading to blue-green to green to the color of the unsubmerged banks.

Now you are ready to assemble your lake permanently, after staining the bottom side of the glass. There are almost as many methods of staining the glass as there are ways of getting trapped into marriage. Kumferman recommends staining both sides of the glass with alcohol color. I've had satisfactory results airbrushing a very thin blue lacquer mixture to the underside of the glass. Others use oils in turps. Regardless of the method used, don't overdo it. Remember, you're supposed to be able to look down through this glass and see the bottom.

Put the stained glass in place and screw the bottom plywood cutout in

position, making sure the bottom contours match those of the upper banks.

Another variation of the glass method of building a pond in this manner is shown in fig. 8-15. In this method, the lake bottom is built first and is permanently fixed to the railroad benchwork. All plasterwork and painting of the lake bottom is completed; then the stained glass is placed on supports and the plaster banks are built up around the outer edges of the glass, following the contours of the bottom. There is one big disadvantage to this type of construction: it is too permanent. If the glass surface is cracked or broken by dropped tools or a heavy locomotive plunging off a nearby bridge, it will be necessary to rip out the upper banks of the lake completely to replace the glass. In the "sandwich" type of glass lake, replacement of the glass in case of breakage is a simple matter of undoing the screws holding the bottom in place and slipping in a new lake surface.

The glass method of building a lake lends itself to detail. The most attractive addition is the pier or wharf. Part of the wharf is constructed to rest on the lake bottom, underneath the glass surface. A matching structure rests on top of the glass, as shown in fig. 8-16. The illusion is that the pilings supporting the wharf extend down beneath the lake's surface and can be seen through the murky water.

Before closing out the discussion of this method of building a lake, let's take a look at the types of glass most suitable for this type of camouflage. Several kinds are available, and they may vary slightly from one section of the country to another, depending upon the source of supply. The one most often referred to is cyanite glass. It has one side smooth, while the other side is rippled in a pattern that very closely resembles waves on a small lake slightly ruffled by a breeze. If this type is used, obviously the wavy side should be up and the smooth side to the bottom of the lake.

There is another type of this so-called "ripple" or office glass. It has an irregular, wavy pattern to both sides; one side is slightly rougher than the other. Then there is still another type of "office" glass entirely *unsuit-*

able for lake construction. It has a small geometrical pattern that looks very much like a closely packed collection of asterisks or small stars molded in its surface. Any glass that has such a geometrical pattern will not make a realistic lake or river.

These various types of office glass are more easily obtainable in the larger towns and cities at glass firms or lumberyards. Railroaders in smaller communities may find it difficult to locate a source of supply. If this is the case, the modeler can follow Kumferman's method of using ordinary, smooth windowpane glass. Larry made his own ripples. He first sprayed the desired shades of blues and greens on both sides of the glass. After the color had dried, he sprayed both sides again, this time using a clear plastic spray. Larry used clear Krylon from a self-spray can. By using the right pressure at the right distance and spraying the Krylon on generously, he was able to create his own "ripple" effect. He points out that a stream of air, such as you might get from an airbrush spray, should be directed over the wet Krylon until the plastic is dry. Otherwise, the ripples tend to smooth out as the plastic dries. If an airbrush is not available, any fairly gentle stream of air will help — such as one from a vacuum cleaner, or an electric fan. In a pinch you can get the ripple effect by blowing air from your mouth onto the wet surface. Larry's method is described in the "Mill Pond" article in the book *The HO Railroad That Grows.*

Another variation of the glass lake method is to build the bottom and banks by sandwiching the glass between laminated layers of celotex cut in wavy, irregular lines to simulate an irregular bank, as shown in fig. 8-17.

Painted plaster method

Probably the cheapest and fastest method of building a river or lake is to use rough plaster to model the banks and smooth plaster for the water surface. All details, including ripples, are modeled directly into the plaster; consequently the water can be constructed at the same time as the rest of the scenery. After the plaster has dried, it is colored. Then several coats of shellac or a very high-gloss varnish are added to give it a wet look. Obviously this method requires a little more artistic effort than others.

One of the many advantages of using plaster to imitate water is the fact that stones and rocks can be pressed down into it while it is wet. This gives the impression that the water is flowing around the rocks. In some other methods, such as the painted plywood river, rocks set on the river appear to be floating on top of the water unless the modeler cuts a hole in the plywood. In using the plaster method to create a river, Wakefield recommends construction of the banks first, complete with paint job. Then the actual flow of the water is added.

Some modelers prefer to use a coarser-textured plaster for the banks and a very smooth plaster for the water. Regardless of your choice, it provides a much more pleasing contrast between water and earth if the banks of the stream are modeled in a rugged manner, with numerous outcroppings of rocks and with earth or rock slides between the jutting stones.

Wakefield advises the use of some form of screening between the banks as the base for the plaster water. This screening can range from something like ¼"-mesh hardware cloth (O scale) to ordinary fine-mesh window screening (HO). It should have some extra support underneath, such as 1 x 2 batten strips inserted across the bays between the horizontal structural members of the grid, as shown in fig. 8-19. These supports help keep the base of the river level. Unsupported

Art Schmidt.

8-18 Gordon Odegard's water and rock on the Tidewater Central are both made of plaster, but the water has a coat of varnish. The bottom of the plastic tugboat was sawed off.

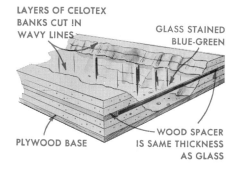

LAYERS OF CELOTEX BANKS CUT IN WAVY LINES

GLASS STAINED BLUE-GREEN

PLYWOOD BASE

WOOD SPACER IS SAME THICKNESS AS GLASS

8-17 Celotex riverbanks.

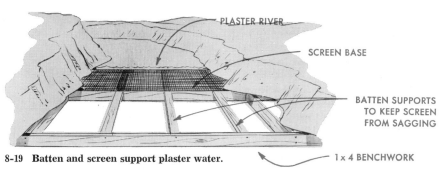

PLASTER RIVER

SCREEN BASE

BATTEN SUPPORTS TO KEEP SCREEN FROM SAGGING

1 x 4 BENCHWORK

8-19 Batten and screen support plaster water.

81

screen wire might tend to sag sadly in the middle with the weight of the wet plaster, and you'd end up with a saucer-shaped top level of water — obviously an impossibility.

Using your fingers and a wet paintbrush as modeling tools, mold the wet plaster mix over the wire screening to represent flowing water. If the river is a large one, include an island or two, elongated to the flow of the water. Mud flats, which can be cluttered with broomstraw "reeds," can appear at certain spots. Pebbles, representing large rocks that have tumbled into the stream, can be pressed into the wet plaster water. Rippled effects where the water flows over a shallow bottom can be reproduced by stippling the plaster.

Some of the most realistic plaster water I've ever seen can be found on the Wolverine Model Railroad Club's fine layout in the Detroit Historical Museum. Builders of the Detroit layout achieved an unusual rippled effect in their plaster water by scribing a series of overlapping circles in the wet plaster, as shown in fig. 8-20. A color photo of the Wolverine layout appears in fig. 8-2.

The rippled effect of the water is similar to what you might find on a very still lake or slowly moving river when the surface has been broken by a pebble tossed into it, or a splash has been made by a large fish breaking water. Ripples such as these spread outward, strike the banks of the lake, and "bounce back" over themselves. This is illustrated in fig. 8-20.

Creating ripples in plaster takes a little experimentation on a scrap piece of plywood. If you intend using this method, the plaster used should be fairly fast-setting and should be mixed to a soupier consistency than that used in other scenic effects. This is to allow the scribed lines representing the ripples to smooth out before setting. Plaster mixed too dry will result in a ripple line that is too deep and sharp, as illustrated in fig. 8-21.

Where a pebble representing a rock has been inserted in the plaster, there should be ripples in the water's surface. These ripples can be modeled by using the fingers.

After the plaster water has hardened, it is ready for the painting. The entire river should be painted at one setting, so allow yourself plenty of time. It's not a project to start just an hour before bedtime. Attempting to paint the water's surface piecemeal is likely to result in a checkerboard effect because a difference in tone will show where you leave off the paint job one time and take up the next.

The entire stream can be painted a medium cloudy blue. Along the banks where the water is shallow, work in

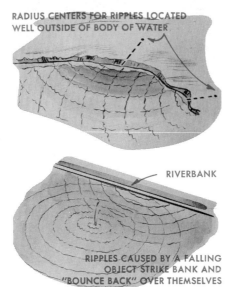

8-20 Ripple location in plaster water.

8-21 If plaster mix is too thick, ripples will not flow together after cutting them. See also figs. 8-2 and 8-28.

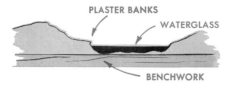

8-22 Plaster lake bed can be shallow, say about 1".

8-23 Depressed area is filled in.

some brownish tones with the blue. Toward the deeper part of the river, work in deeper blues. Where the water is rough, at the bottoms of small falls and around rapids and stones in the water where the water is roughened, the action can be heightened by dry-brushing the roughened surface with white.

After the painted plaster water has had a chance to dry thoroughly, give it at least two coats of a high-gloss clear varnish — or shellac. Be sure to cover only that part of the plaster which is supposed to be water with the glossy varnish, leaving exposed sandbars and islands in a flat dry color. This heightens the contrast.

Waterglass method

The waterglass method of creating rivers or lakes is very similar to that used in the plastic method. Waterglass is a substance consisting of sodium silicate, or sometimes potassium silicate, dissolved in water to form a thick, clear, syrupy liquid. Sometimes it is a combination of the two silicates, sodium and potassium. It is also known as "soluble glass." It is used as a cement, as a protective coating, as a preservative for eggs, and for hardening surgical dressings.

To form a lake by this method, the modeler can build a shallow, depressed lake bed in his scenery. Follow the same procedures as outlined for the creation of the plastic lake as far as modeling and painting the lake bed. (See fig. 8-22.) Then pour in a generous coating of the waterglass and allow it to dry naturally without application of heat. It may be necessary to add a second, even a third, coating in the center of the lake, as there may be a tendency for the waterglass to shrink as it dries, leaving a depression in the center of the pond as shown in fig. 8-23. Of course, the surface of the lake should be level, so this dip in the "surface" can be filled in with additional waterglass poured IN THE DEPRESSED AREA ONLY.

Frankly, I have never had much luck with the use of waterglass in any phase of model railroading and do not recommend its use. It is subject to changes in humidity, and when it becomes old, it tends to crack and curl.

Sheet plywood method

The use of sheet plywood, properly surfaced and painted, is another quick, easy method of creating an artificial river. Like the shellacked plaster method, it may require a bit more artistic skill on the part of the builder. If the modeler lives in a humid climate, it's a good idea to shellac both sides of the plywood before starting construction, to prevent buckling of the outer sheets of the veneer.

The plywood, either ¼" or ½" thickness, serves as the surface of the river. It is screwed in place at the desired water level, above the grids forming your table. This method is almost the same as the painted plaster method — the difference is that screen wire and plaster are not applied to the flat plywood surface. See fig. 8-25.

If it is necessary to use more than one piece of plywood in the formation of a lengthy river, the line where the two sheets of wood butt together should be filled with plastic wood or putty and sanded smooth. Nothing looks more unrealistic than a ruler-straight line running across what is supposed to be flowing water.

Now, it would take a real Rembrandt to paint the perfectly smooth surface of the flat plywood to resemble water. You must create some 3-D ripples on the surface. I've found that plastic wood, applied in wavy lines ranging in thickness from 1⁄16" to 1⁄8", does the job. Before applying the plastic wood ripples, anything such as dead tree trunks, rocks, and other debris which might logically protrude out of the water should be inserted in the plywood. These objects should be fitted into holes, either bored or sawed, in the plywood; otherwise they might appear to be floating on the water's surface.

Be sure to model churning water or ripples in the wake of those objects which break through the surface. This can be done by stippling the plastic wood with a brush. Most plastic woods are held together with a lacquer-base glue or adhesive, and it is a good idea to dampen the brush with lacquer thinner occasionally while stippling.

Clint Grant.

8-24 Ripples at Coyote Creek on my railroad are made with plastic wood coated on plywood surface and painted with varying hues of blues, greens, and brownish greens capped with white dry-brushed ripple tops. High-gloss varnish makes river look wet.

After the water surface is complete, construct the plaster riverbanks down to the water's edge using your favorite method of construction.

When the plastic wood has dried, the river is ready for the paint job. Use the same procedure as described for painting the shellacked plaster river — deeper blues and greens toward the center and deeper parts of the river, gradually changing to greens and light tans near the water's edge. Dry-brush the ruffled water around the stones with white to represent whitecaps or froth.

After the paint has dried completely, apply several thick coats of the gloss-

iest, shiniest clear varnish you can find, allowing suitable drying time between coats. The illusion of water can be heightened by adding a blue-green tint to a couple of coats of the varnish.

Pigment-type paint, such as artist's tube oil colors, will kill the transparency of the varnish. Aniline dyes can be used to tint the varnish, but there's a problem here, since aniline dye is soluble only in alcohol and is not compatible with varnish. This problem can be solved by dissolving a minimum amount of the desired dyes in alcohol, then adding this mixture to a larger amount of turpentine — with considerable stirring. This dye-al-

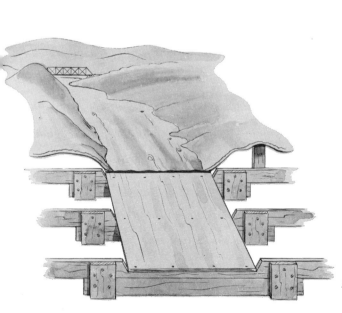

8-25 Rivers will often look better if you build them below regular grid level of tables. Be sure to use a strong method of construction, depending on location.

8-26

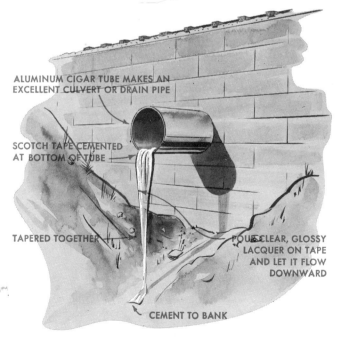

ALUMINUM CIGAR TUBE MAKES AN EXCELLENT CULVERT OR DRAIN PIPE

SCOTCH TAPE CEMENTED AT BOTTOM OF TUBE

TAPERED TOGETHER

POUR CLEAR, GLOSSY LACQUER ON TAPE AND LET IT FLOW DOWNWARD

CEMENT TO BANK

Linn Westcott.

8-27 Leslie White's churned water was made by drawing the plaster up into points and tipping them with white. Trestle is copy of logging trestle near Seattle. HO pike is in Chisford, Virginia, at White's farm. Note painted background 8 feet away.

cohol-turpentine mixture then is stirred into the varnish, and the resulting mixture is applied to the painted plywood river.

Real water as water

If real water is to be used, an absolutely leakproof container must be constructed. This can be done by building a metallic tank, or by building a lake bed of concrete or Portland cement. All rivers or lakes have twist-

ing, curling banks, and to build a metallic tank in the irregular shape of such a body of water would tax the craftsmanship of the best worker in metal. If a tank is to be used, it could be constructed in the general shape of the river or lake, either square or rectangular, and waterproofed concrete banks could be built down into the tank to make the irregular shoreline. The tank can be formed of heavy-gauge steel painted inside and out

with two coats of asphalt to make it leakproof. A third coat should be added inside and a fine layer of aquarium gravel should be sprinkled on it to give it a sandy appearance.

Another method of constructing a waterproofed lake bed is to build it of Portland cement. Obviously such a project must be strongly supported in the layout framework, or else it might come tumbling down some dark night and drown all the mice in the cellar — or attic. Use either metal lathing or ¼"-mesh hardware cloth to form the bed of the lake roughly. Cover the supporting wire with a mixture of 1 part Portland cement to 5 parts sand. Spread the mixture thickly over the support. Cover the cement with wet cloths to keep it from drying too rapidly and cracking. This, when dry, can be waterproofed by covering it with TWO COATS of a soupy mixture of pure Portland cement. When dry, it should be painted and water should be added.

It was fairly easy for S scale modeler Dick Houghton to build a real-water lake on his Belmont Lines. His layout was in a partly excavated basement, and some of his track ran over unexcavated prototype earth. He just scooped a depression in the dirt for his lake. Then he dampened the earth (this kept the cement from drying too fast) and trowled the mix of Portland cement and sand over the lake bed to the thickness of about an inch. Two coats of soupy mixture of pure old Portland were then brushed over the concrete to make it waterproof. After 4 hours of drying (after the last waterproofing coat), the lake was covered with wet newspapers to retard drying. After 2 or 3 days of this slow-dry process, the lake was ready for water.

Dick colored his water blue by mixing ½ teaspoonful of copper sulfate into 2 gallons of water. (Incidentally, if copper sulfate is used to color the water, you need not worry about it being a watering place for bugs — that compound is used as an insect spray by gardeners. It is a poison, so take care.) He has taken advantage of the real water to include a real water-wheel for his mill by the lakeside — one of the advantages of using the real thing. An even more ambitious project would involve using real water in the working locks of a model canal.

J. S. Bordeleau of Montreal added a couple of innovations to his real-water lake. In order to keep the water from becoming stagnant, he planted various types of aquarium plants in it. His lake is contained in an asphalt-treated galvanized tank. Bordeleau whipped the evaporation problem by continuously feeding fresh water to his lake through a rubber tube from a

8-28 **Closeup of ripples by Wolverine Model Railroad Club members at Detroit Historical Museum. These are made in plaster while still quite fluid, then coated with color and varnish or plastic paint later. See also full-color photo, fig. 8-2.**

gravity tank placed 5 feet above the layout.

He gets realistic effects from this scheme of replenishing the evaporation by running the water from the tube over a mill waterwheel, down through a winding creek, over a waterfall, through some rapids, and into the lake. There is a small vent at the end of the lake to take care of overflow in case he forgets to cut off the water supply from the gravity tank.

Blue mirror method

Construction of a lake using a blue mirror to imitate the water's surface is done exactly the same way as the ripple glass method — with one exception. Since the mirror is NOT transparent, it isn't necessary to cut an opening in the lower piece of plywood nor to construct the bottom of the lake.

Just put the mirror on supports at the desired water level and run the plaster banks down to the edge. Paint the banks earth color, and you're in business.

Quite a few model railroaders obtain a realistic effect of water pouring out of drain pipes and culverts by combining Scotch tape and clear lacquer or shellac, as shown in fig. 8-26. The Scotch tape is stuck in place inside, at the bottom of the culvert. Taper it together as it falls downward to the lake surface — or rocks below. Then flow many coats of clear lacquer down the tape to give it a glossy effect of falling water.

DETAIL heightens the realism of model railroad scenery. The less scenery that is included on the model railroad layout, the better it must be. When there is little scenery, the critical eye of the observer lingers longer on one particular piece of landscaping. And if it is lacking in detail, it is lacking in realism. Fortunately this works out in favor of the modeler with the small layout. Obviously it is easier to superdetail a small 4 x 8-foot pike than it is to superdetail a king-size layout.

Thus far we have dealt largely with modeling the natural scene, but there are certain man-made features of the countryside that become such a part of the natural scene that they cannot be ignored. For instance, such things as a stone tunnel portal or a brick or stone retaining wall set in the side of a mountain are so much a part of the earth surrounding them that they must be modeled right along with the surrounding terrain.

This also holds true of such things as culverts and bridge and trestle piers. It is often best to model them in the plaster along with the earth surrounding them. Other details such as tunnel telltales, telephone poles, and signal semaphores can be added after the plastering is complete.

One of the most neglected details in model scenery is the grade crossing, where the tracks and a street or highway intersect.

Many railroaders are content to tack a strip of shirt cardboard or illustration board between the tracks, or daub a little plaster between the rails, and call it a grade crossing. Some don't even go to this trouble. These modelers run their street right up to the track, chopping it off there and leaving the rails sticking up in the air about a scale foot, expecting the traffic to flow over them somehow smoothly to reach the other side. Ignoring the basic requirements of a grade crossing is not only rough on scale characters in Model T Fords attempting to cross the tracks, but it also gives the eye of the observer quite a jolt.

Highway crossings at their best are rough affairs, even in the prototype. Paul Larson, former editor of MODEL RAILROADER, once pointed out, "Our best brains — for over a century — have conceived, built, and rebuilt some 231,000 highway crossings along

Clint Grant.

9-1 Earl Cochran built this beet loader on a plywood base. Later he gave it to me and I hid the base edges with plaster and cemented gravel over the surfaces.

a quarter-million miles of railroad route with one singular feature. They are all rough!" So, why make it tough on your scale characters by making them bounce across our already oversize rails?

Actually, the highway crossing offers one of the best spots on the layout for superdetailing with a minimum of effort.

There are about five basic types of highway crossing: (1) timbers or planks; (2) rolled asphalt; (3) poured concrete; (4) fill of earth or stone; (5) precast concrete slabs.

There are about four general rules that must be observed in constructing grade crossings, whether they be in the prototype or in the model:

● Adequate flangeway must be provided — 1/16" is about right for HO gauge; 3/32" for O gauge.

● Top of the material used for the crossing between rails must be kept at railtop level — or slightly below it. (Extreme care must be taken to observe these two rules in model construction to insure a smooth flow of rail traffic across the crossing.)

● Practically all types of crossings have the ends of any filling *between* the tracks beveled so that dragging

equipment will ride up and over with minimum damage to equipment and the crossing.

● Last, but not least, the crossing must be exactly as wide as the highway or road.

Keeping all these rules in mind, let's discuss simple ways of modeling each type of crossing.

Timber or plank type

On the prototype, this kind of crossing is usually built of creosoted 4 x 8 timbers laid on furring strips and bolted or screwed to the ties. In modelwork, pine, basswood, or balsa stripwood can be used. Stripwood 1/16" x 3/32" is best for HO; 1/8" x 3/16" for O scale. Cut the stripwood as long as the highway is wide, bevel the ends, shim with cardboard to *almost* railtop level, and fix in place with either cement or escutcheon pins. Stain with turpentine and burnt umber. See fig. 9-2.

Asphalt crossing

This is a very common type in the prototype and can be modeled by filling between the rails with plastic wood or plaster. While the mixture is still soft, press in the proper flangeways. Pass a car or locomotive through the crossing to make sure that the flangeways are deep enough. Stain the surface to match the approaching highway. See fig. 9-3.

Fill crossing

This sort of crossing is most often found on little-used roads where the light traffic can't justify heavier construction. The road is graded to railtop level and cinders, dirt, or gravel is dumped between the rails. Mainline crossings of this type usually have guardrails or timber flangeway guards. In modeling this type of crossing, cement two lengths of $\frac{1}{16}'' \times \frac{1}{16}''$ stripwood between rails to serve as flangeway guards; then fill in between with plaster if it's a dirt crossing, or cement ballast in place almost to railtop level if it is to be a gravel crossing.

Concrete crossing

On prototype railroads, this type of crossing is usually found only at spots where highway traffic is unusually heavy. Lengths of rail are usually set in place to guard the flangeways and concrete is poured between them. That's the same procedure used in modeling this crossing — except that we use plaster instead of concrete. Plaster also is placed on the outside of the tracks leading to the highway. See fig. 9-5.

Precast concrete crossing

This type of crossing is also found where highway traffic is heavy, but where there might be reason to tear it up occasionally for track maintenance. It is made of precast slabs of concrete 4" to 6" thick bolted to the crossties in much the same manner as the plank type of crossing. In modelwork, strips of balsa or basswood can be cut, beveled, and painted a concrete gray to imitate the prototype.

Other details such as the conventional crossbuck or the more elaborate electrical flasher warning system, crossing gates (either operating or dummy), cattle guards, and fences can be added to complete the realism of the highway grade-crossing scene.

ALMOST as ignored as the grade crossing on our model railroads are the roads and highways that lead to crossings. Roads are as much a part of the scenery as the cliffs and valleys on the model railroad, and should be included in the basic plaster scenery. Many modelers are prone to build elaborate trackside structures to serve boxcars and other rolling stock that may be shuttled off to their sidings, but they seem to forget completely that there must be roads over which local traffic can reach these buildings to pick up and drop freight.

Roads and highways crisscrossing and running parallel to the railroads are as much a part of the railway scene as the crossties and rails themselves. Only in very remote regions, such as where the old Rio Grande puffs through the craggy vastness of mountain gorges between Durango and Silverton, are highways alongside the tracks lacking. Even in these primitive areas, roads and highways begin to appear out of the forests as the train approaches towns, dude ranches, and other centers of civilization.

One modeler who made a study of roads is M. B. Wakefield. He points out that five types of road are commonly found in our national scene today. They are: the dirt road, gravel road, and the asphalt, the concrete, and the concrete-asphalt types. There are other types, such as the wooden brick-block, common brick, stone, and the now almost-extinct wooden log or plank road. However, these last-named would require so much detailed work to make them appear realistic that they are impractical in the model scene.

The principal rule in road construction is that every road must *appear* to be going somewhere. A highway that leads away from a railroad station or freight depot only to stop abruptly at the foot of a mountain serves no practical purpose and doesn't appear realistic at all. Let the road either wind around the base of the mountain or climb along the side and then disappear beyond. You may even lead off the front edge of the table.

The conventional construction method for all five of the most common types of highway is generally the same: see figs. 9-8 and 9-9. Flat pieces of scrap lumber slightly wider than the desired width of the road or highway are tacked or screwed to the benchwork. These pieces of planking serve as the baseboard for the road. Wire mesh is then tacked *over* the top of this flat surface, allowing about $\frac{1}{16}''$ or $\frac{1}{8}''$ air space *between* the wire and wood baseboard. (Without this air space, plaster has a tendency to pull away from the flat surface of the baseboards and crack.) See fig. 9-8.

Allow the screen to dip (to form roadside ditches), then curve upward and join the surrounding plaster scenery. The screen roadbed is then covered with a smooth coat of plaster. While the plaster is still wet, smooth it with a flat piece of wood dipped in water occasionally to prevent plaster from sticking to it and pulling away from the screen. This first step can be basic in practically all types of highway construction. Don't neglect to add the gravel shoulders found on modern-vintage roads and main highways.

9-2 Plank crossing.

9-3 Asphalt crossing.

9-4 Fill crossing.

9-5 Poured concrete crossing.

9-6 Precast concrete crossing.

K. Phillips Kallman.

9-7 Road and railroad cross in a cut on this NYSME scene by M. B. Wakefield.

Hard-shell method for roads

Those who have erected scenery without using screen wire may feel the plywood-and-screen undersupport for roads is going to a lot of extra work. It is the traditional way it has been done. Hard-shell users, however, find they can build roads by hard-shell methods just like any other scenery. The only real problem is to get the road surface flat. This can be done by erecting plywood, Homasote, Upson board or other temporary surfaces under the road area and covering this surface with plastic wrapping film (so plaster does not stick to the surface). Soaked paper-towel or cloth strips are then laid over the forms and after this first coating is hard the top layer or actual road surface is added in the same crowned shape as with traditional construction. Modelers who have used both the traditional and the hard-shell methods say the new way is strong and that it saves time and cost.

If the undersupport forms are re-

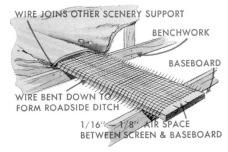

9-8 Screen for plaster road.

moved, they can be used to build roads elsewhere. Large flat areas, like the station plaza, may require a little extra thickness with self-supporting plaster because plaster is not as strong in flat surfaces as in undulating terrain.

Road width

Plank roads and very early auto highways of concrete were only 8 feet wide and were located along one side of the center line of the (often 66-foot) public right of way. Occasional unpaved wide spots on the other side of center were used for overtaking or meeting other vehicles.

Many highways of the twenties were only 16 to 20 feet wide over all, but modern highways and business streets are built at least 12 feet wide per driving lane. Business-district sidewalks are typically 10 feet wide or more, and in the better districts they may have trees either planted in open squares just back from the curb or in wood pots.

A "40-foot" or "60-foot" residential street is by no means all pavement. From the center out a typical U. S. residential street, regardless of overall width, includes a pavement of 16 feet or more, usually but not always a curb and gutter, a "parking" area of grass, and a 4- or sometimes 3- or 5-foot sidewalk. Almost always 1 or 2 feet of the public property extends beyond the sidewalk edge into the front lawns.

Modelers often build pavements a little underscale in width to save space. If this is done, be sure not to put large vehicles in the area and give the ruse away.

Now let's consider road types.

Dirt road

Naturally this type of trafficway is much narrower than the well-kept paved road. It is often deeply rutted from wheels passing over it in rainy weather. To create this illusion in the model, run the wheels of a model car (approximately the same scale as your track) through the plaster road while it is still damp. Let the ruts twist and turn and cross and crisscross each other. Actually this type of road never needs the baseboard construction described earlier, since it can so easily be modeled directly on the existing terrain.

Since the earth road is usually made of the same soil as that around it, the

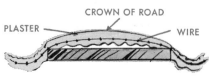

9-9 Road with crown.

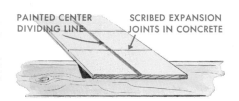

9-10 Road without crown.

coloring should use the same mixture. If the road is badly rutted, dark brown stain in the ruts and light brown on the crests will give desired contrasts.

Grass and weeds usually grow in the raised area between ruts and close to each side of the roadway. Of course, a freshly scraped road will have no ruts nor weeds.

Gravel road

After the finish coat of plaster has been applied over the hard shell or screen and while it is still impressionable and damp, sprinkle a very fine grade of ballast or bird gravel over the surface and press it gently into the plaster with a flat block of wood; dampen the block frequently. After the plaster has dried, brush the surplus gravel into the roadside ditches. Gravel roads may range in color from a light gray to various shades of light browns. For the types of gravel roads found in the Southwest, a thin stain of yellow ocher with occasional darker spots of raw sienna would be about right.

Asphalt road

Again we use the baseboard-screen method, but in applying the plaster we build a slight crown down the middle of the road, fig. 9-9, and bevel the edges of the highway slightly. The crown or curve of the road's surface should not be too pronounced, just barely enough to be noticeable, and can be achieved by merely putting the plaster on a little thicker down the middle of the road and allowing it to slope gently to the beveled edges. After the plaster has dried, paint it a dead deep slate-gray shade. Westcott has pointed out that "black" pavements are really far from black unless freshly laid or wet. Often a medium gray will look just right where a deep black will be an eyesore on a model layout. The reasoning for this is not just a matter of more natural coloring but also because all colors tend to look darker indoors than in nature. Linn lightens all his coloring a little to compensate for this.

A yellow, or white, stripe down the middle of the highway is the finishing touch.

Concrete highway

Plaster over the screen wire and board base is smoothed out as flat as

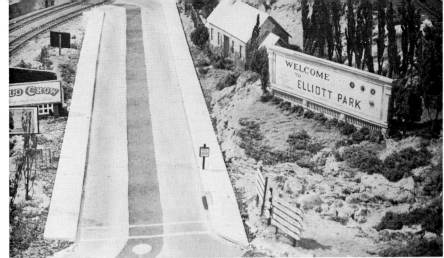

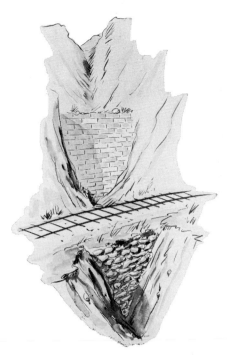

9-11 NYSME road with abandoned trolley-car strip.

K. Phillips Kallman.

9-12 Slide-stopping walls.

possible for a concrete highway. While the plaster is still damp, use a fine knife point and scribe the horizontal expansion joints about a scale 20 feet apart. See fig. 9-10.

There is another method of building a concrete highway that is perhaps a bit faster. The baseboard itself, without any screen-wire covering or plaster, serves as the highway. Hide all attaching nailheads and countersunk screws holding the plank highway to the benchwork with putty or plastic wood. Sand absolutely smooth to hide all evidence of wood grain, and paint.

Concrete highways should be a concrete gray and may have either black or yellow lane stripes painted down the middle. Joints between the slabs of concrete (expansion joints) can be scribed into the wood before painting. Thin wash streaks of raw umber and lampblack stroked in with a fine brush lengthwise on the highway may represent tire marks and streaks of grease and oil that accumulate on all well-traveled roads.

Concrete-asphalt highway

This is a common type of trafficway found around most cities. Usually this type of road has two concrete strips running parallel with a center strip of asphalt. In communities where streetcar operation is still the thing, the asphalt strip may contain tracks; in cases where the streetcars have been abandoned in favor of bus operation, the asphalt strip may cover the old tram tracks. In building this type of highway, use the baseboard type of construction (fig. 9-10); it may or may not be covered with plaster. The support should be a scale 60 feet wide if sidewalks are to run along each side of the street. If sidewalks are not desired, the width can be reduced to about 44 scale feet.

If the bare baseboards are to represent the highway, sanding and painting are all that is required. Of course, the middle section representing the

asphalt strip is painted a deep slate gray, and the concrete strips a cement gray. If sidewalks are desired, stripwood ⅛" (actual) by a scale 8 feet wide can be tacked along the edges and painted a lighter shade of concrete gray.

Since the asphalt strip probably will appear more realistic if it has more texture, plaster is probably the best surface for its construction. In this case, if sidewalks are desired, they can be used to secure any wire-screen covering over the baseboard.

ANOTHER interesting detail that is usually best to construct while slapping on the plaster scenery is the retaining wall. Retaining walls on real railroads are used both above and below track level; in some cases, in both places at the same location. Those placed *above* track level pre-

vent earth or rocks from sliding onto the tracks; those placed *below* track level either fill a low place or are used to prevent the supporting earth from washing or sliding from under the tracks. See fig. 9-12.

There are several types of retaining wall. The most common are studded timbers, cribbing, stone, rock or brick, and cast concrete. For my money, either the cribbing or the stone retaining wall (fig. 9-13) is most attractive in modelwork.

The cribbing-type retaining wall can be built of square stripwood — ⅛"

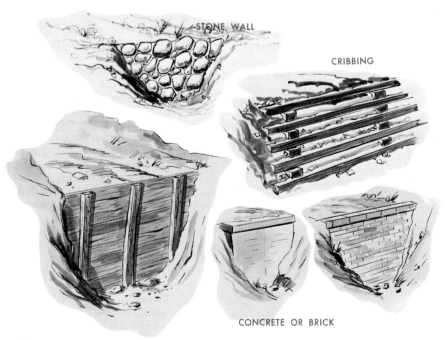

STONE WALL

CRIBBING

PLANK RETAINING WALL

CONCRETE OR BRICK

9-13 Types of retaining walls.

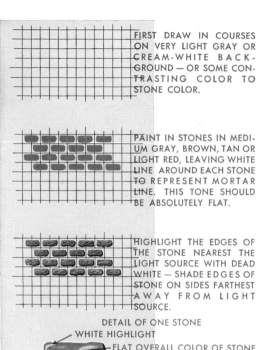

FIRST DRAW IN COURSES ON VERY LIGHT GRAY OR CREAM-WHITE BACKGROUND — OR SOME CONTRASTING COLOR TO STONE COLOR.

PAINT IN STONES IN MEDIUM GRAY, BROWN, TAN OR LIGHT RED, LEAVING WHITE LINE AROUND EACH STONE TO REPRESENT MORTAR LINE. THIS TONE SHOULD BE ABSOLUTELY FLAT.

HIGHLIGHT THE EDGES OF THE STONE NEAREST THE LIGHT SOURCE WITH DEAD WHITE — SHADE EDGES OF STONE ON SIDES FARTHEST AWAY FROM LIGHT SOURCE.

DETAIL OF ONE STONE
WHITE HIGHLIGHT
FLAT OVERALL COLOR OF STONE
SLIGHTLY DEEPER SHADE
DEEPEST TONE OF FLAT BLACK
IMPORTANT — MAKE SURE ALL HIGHLIGHTS ARE ON SAME SIDE - SHADOWS ON OPPOSITE SIDE.

9-14 Masonry faked with paint.

in HO and ¼" in O scale. The drawing at the far right in fig. 9-13 shows cribbing construction.

There are several ways of modeling the brick or stone retaining wall. A number of fine brick and stone walls, portals, abutments, and the like are available in cast plastic ready to set into the plaster in the proper places. Naturally you can change their coloring to match other stonework nearby. For those who want a brick wall, there are also several other excellent readymade products available at the hobby shop. Suydam offers an embossed fiberboard brick material that is very realistic. Northeastern markets brick-embossed sheetwood. Either can be cut to shape and placed in the plaster scenery. Holgate & Reynolds in Evanston, Illinois, markets a plastic sheet with embossed bricks, as well as a stone sheet. Vollmer offers cast plastic sheets of brick and roof material that are exact matches for the Vollmer structures in case you wish to modify

V-SHAPED CUTTING TOOL FOR SCRIBING

ARCH MAY BE SAWED OUT FOR TUNNEL PORTAL

"BATTLESHIP" LINOLEUM MOUNTED ON WOOD BLOCK

OR BLOCK MAY BE USED FOR RETAINING WALL.

9-15 Carved masonry.

them or match them with retaining walls and the like.

The "do-it-yourself" boy has two courses open. He can carve his retaining wall directly into a stretch of plaster which has been molded flat in his scenery, either while it is wet or after it has dried. Or, he can carve or paint a stone wall on a piece of flat, soft white pine and set it in place in the plaster earth. If properly shadowed and highlighted, it is almost impossible to tell a flat, painted stone wall from a 3-D carved wall at a distance of 2 or 3 feet. The few simple rules of highlighting and shading painted stones are shown in fig. 9-14.

There is still another method of making a very realistic stone retaining wall. That is by carving the stonework in a linoleum block (fig. 9-15) and pressing it into place while the plaster scenery is still wet. Linoleum of the proper type can be obtained at art supply stores. It is about ¼" thick and usually comes mounted on wooden blocks. It is used by artists to carve linoleum-block cuts. A V-shaped linoleum cutting tool or scribe makes the job easier. It can also be obtained at an art supply store.

The scribed mortar lines are painted white or the desired color of the mortar (some construction firms use a dark, black, or gray mortar); then the raised stonework is painted a contrasting shade, either brown or gray.

Linoleum blocks are not only handy for building retaining walls but are also excellent material for home-grown tunnel portals. The arch of the tunnel portal is cut out on a jig saw; then the mortar lines and stones are cut into the linoleum surface (fig. 9-15). I have two such portals on my layout.

Westcott says he is a lazy modeler when it comes to carving anything twice over. Instead, he makes a rubber mold of the first side of a wall, bridge, or other brick or masonry feature and casts as many duplicates of it as he needs. You can get some ideas of how to do this from the material on rock casting in chapter 4.

The culvert is another type of man-made detail that must be included in the original plaster scenery, since it must appear to be embedded in the earth. A culvert is simply a transverse drain or waterway under a highway or a railroad for the simple purpose of allowing water to flow freely from one side to the other of the tracks or roadway without flowing over it. Culverts differ from bridges. A culvert is an opening through the roadbed with a depth of roadbed *above* it, whereas a bridge replaces an entire section of roadbed. Bridges usually consist of a substructure and a superstructure, but a culvert is a single structure.

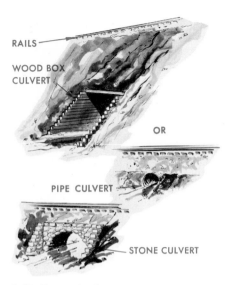

RAILS
WOOD BOX CULVERT
OR
PIPE CULVERT
STONE CULVERT

9-16 Types of culverts.

There are three basic types of culverts: pipe, box, and arch (fig. 9-16). These three types are further divided as to size and material as follows:

Type	Materials	Size range
Pipe (may be round or egg-shaped)	Vitrified clay	6" to 36" dia.
	*Concrete	24" to 108" dia.
	Wood	24" to 72" dia.
	Cast Iron	12" to 48" dia.
	*Corrugated steel	Up to 108" dia.
Box	*Wood (treated)	12" to 72" sq.
	*Concrete	Large (tall as a man)
	Stone	Generally small
Arch	*Concrete	All sizes
	Masonry (stone, brick)	All sizes
	*Corrugated steel	18" x 11" to 72" x 44"

*Modern construction generally limited to these types.

For those wishing to really go in strong for superdetailed culverts, I refer them to National Model Railroad Association's data sheet D6a, issued in October 1955 and compiled by those veterans of the lilliputian rails, Hobson, Towers, and Ravenscroft. This data sheet is composed of eight pages containing all the engineering data needed to construct almost any type of culvert. It is profusely illustrated with fine engineering drawings.

A few simple rules should be observed in culvert construction:

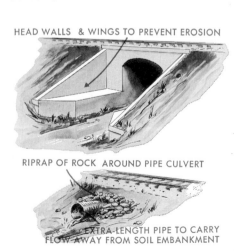

HEAD WALLS & WINGS TO PREVENT EROSION

RIPRAP OF ROCK AROUND PIPE CULVERT

EXTRA-LENGTH PIPE TO CARRY FLOW AWAY FROM SOIL EMBANKMENT

9-17 More culverts.

● Height of the culvert opening is limited by the height of the fill. This is because the earth cover between culvert top and ballast should be at least 3 feet deep, particularly in the case of pipe culverts.

● The span or width of a culvert opening should be sufficient to carry the volume of water to pass under the tracks at maximum flow. In the case of arch or pipe culverts, multiple units allow for large flows.

● Length of the culvert depends upon the width of the base of the embankment, plus gradient and skew angle of the culvert and whether headwalls are to be built. This is best determined by making a cross-section sketch.

Headwalls and wings leading into the culvert are not for mere decoration. They resist erosion and reduce the danger of accumulation of loose material at the culvert openings. However, where space permits in the case of a pipe culvert, extra length of pipe is provided to clear the embankment and carry the water flow away from earth likely to erode. Sometimes stone rubble or riprap is piled around the opening of a pipe culvert to prevent washing or erosion. See fig. 9-17.

The pipe culvert is the simplest of all types to model. Any type of tubing the right scale size can be used. If it is to represent a galvanized metal culvert, paint it aluminum or silver. If it is to be cast iron, paint it black; if concrete, paint it a gray cement color.

If you happen to be a cigar smoker, your problem is solved. Some brands of cigars (very expensive ones) come in individual aluminum metal tubes about 5" to 6" long. These make ideal pipe culverts.

Perhaps you prefer to roll your own and make a corrugated pipe culvert. This can be modeled by shaping some of the corrugated aluminum metal marketed by E. Suydam & Company, Box 55, Duarte, CA 91010. Most hobby shops sell the stuff in sheets. It can be rolled around a dowel of the desired size to give it the proper shape.

The procedure you will follow in installing the culvert differs according to the type of culvert you want and just how far it is to be placed beneath the tracks. If the top of the culvert is to be at the bottom of a steep embankment, quite a distance below trackbed level, simply cut a hole in the screen-wire or paper plaster support, insert the culvert end, and work the plaster around it.

But if the culvert is in a shallow embankment almost directly beneath the bottom of the ties, it may be necessary to cut off the beveled edge of the roadbed and roadbed support in a line parallel to the outer edges of the ties.

INSERT TUBE FOR CULVERT IN HOLE IN SCREEN WIRE AND PLASTER AROUND IT.

SCREEN WIRE TACKED TO WIRE PLASTER SUPPORT

TO INSTALL CULVERT DIRECTLY BENEATH TRACKS, CUT AWAY BEVELED ROADBED WITH CHISEL.

9-18 Culvert installation.

This bevel should be cut away for a distance of about 3 actual inches each side of the center line of the culvert. See fig. 9-18.

I have several large, multiple-opening stone-arch culverts on my layout, made of wood from scotch whisky spacers. These culverts are placed in spots theoretically besieged by flash floods, where the drainage must be almost instantaneous; and the openings are about a scale 18 feet in diameter. These bottle spacers come in mighty handy in many ways for the fellow who likes arches but doesn't have a jigsaw. They are strips of white pine about $5/16$" thick, 2½" wide and 12" to 14" long. They come with four perfectly cut, equally spaced semicircular openings cut in them. They are used to pack imported liquor; the semicircular openings fit around the necks of the bottles to keep them from shifting about in the wooden packing cases while on their way across the stormy Atlantic from dear ol' Scotland. Scribed and painted to resemble stonework, these arches can be used to construct everything from small bridges and large culverts to arch windows in large buildings.

One important rule to keep in mind constantly when adding detail to model railroads is that this detail must be in keeping with the times. If it is a modern railroad that is being modeled, it is permissible to include some old-time construction. This is perfectly logical, since it is possible that the construction crews haven't gotten around to replacing the old with the new. But if it is an old-time railroad that is being modeled, it is definitely not in keeping with its times to include such modern features as con-

crete tunnel portals and steel high-tension towers in the scenery detail.

TUNNEL portals — like culverts and retaining walls — while man-made, fit so snugly into the plaster scenery that it is often best to fit them in place while building the basic scenery. There are four general types of tunnel portals. They are concrete, masonry (stone or brick — or a mixture of the two), timber, and a natural rock bore.

Most modern tunnel portals are of cast concrete construction and may be as simple as an arch, or even a square, opening in a flat-face wall of concrete. On the other hand, some concrete tunnel portals have massive rectangular columns and resemble more the outside of some sort of temple than a mere tunnel portal.

Excellent ready-made tunnel portals in both double-track and single-track widths can be purchased at hobby shops. Alexander Scale Models in particular puts out several excellent tunnel portals cast in plaster. They range from old stone masonry to the more modern concrete type.

Also available are timber portal kits. If the kit-form tunnel portals are not quite exactly what you need on your particular layout, it is quite simple to build one from scratch, using stripwood. On many western railroads, timber tunnel portals are still in use. One thing to keep in mind is that most timber portals are located in a mountainous region near a stand of lumber.

Model portals also can be constructed with plaster casting methods, or by carving them from wood, or carving them directly out of plaster scenery (if it is to represent a rock bore). However, it is not the purpose of this book to give step-by-step detailed construction description of how to scratchbuild a tunnel portal. Rather, it is our purpose to point out a few simple rules to follow when putting tunnel portals in place in the scenery.

Rules governing the placement of tunnel portals on the model layout are simple:

● Before permanently securing the portal, make absolutely certain it clears all types of equipment which will operate through it. (Many make the sad mistake of testing clearances on only a few cars and locomotives only to discover, too late, that the portal will not allow a wrecking crane or big hook, full-length passenger car, rack, or high-cube car to pass through. On curves the clearances are even more difficult to provide, and if you will operate articulated steam locos be sure to allow for the front-end overhang. On double track the clearance between tracks must also be increased greatly on curves.)

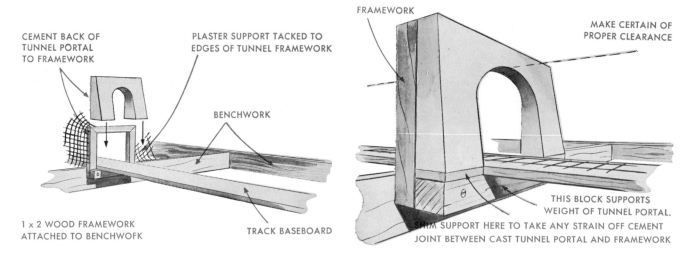

CEMENT BACK OF
TUNNEL PORTAL
TO FRAMEWORK

PLASTER SUPPORT TACKED TO
EDGES OF TUNNEL FRAMEWORK

BENCHWORK

1 x 2 WOOD FRAMEWORK
ATTACHED TO BENCHWOFK

TRACK BASEBOARD

FRAMEWORK

MAKE CERTAIN OF
PROPER CLEARANCE

THIS BLOCK SUPPORTS
WEIGHT OF TUNNEL PORTAL.

SHIM SUPPORT HERE TO TAKE ANY STRAIN OFF CEMENT
JOINT BETWEEN CAST TUNNEL PORTAL AND FRAMEWORK

9-19 Ready-made tunnel portals can be mounted on a block crossing under the roadbed.

● Portals should be fixed securely in the scenery. If they loosen they could dislodge and cause a serious accident to a locomotive. One way to fix a portal in place is to build a framework of wood nailed or screwed to the benchwork as shown in fig. 9-19. The portal can then be glued or cemented to this framework.

● Keep all outside light from reaching the tunnel interior. Railroad tunnels are supposed to be dark, dank, sooty places, and it spoils the realism if light creeps into one from the open side of the mountain next to the wall, or filters from somewhere beneath the mountain. You can stop unwanted light with cardboard baffles and paint any part of the tunnel's interior visible to the eye a flat black.

There is one sort of tunnel portal construction which will be described, since it is actually part of the plaster scenery. It is the rock bore with a portal face of the natural rock alone. This type of tunnel is found only where rock is firm, not easily dislodged, and free from the effects of erosion or frost. The Rockies boast many such tunnels and a few are found in the East as well — wherever rock is firm.

While rock tunnels were created traditionally by the wood-and-wire-screen method, the hard-shell method is so much simpler and quicker that only it will be explained here. You can use molding plaster (or, in a pinch, patching plaster or other gypsum-type plaster) for it, since there is no need for long setting times. The steps are suggested by Westcott with the idea that you can improvise on them for your special needs.

The track-supporting roadbed under the tunnel site should be the full width of the desired tunnel bore plus a bit more. Over this you model, in plaster, the tunnel floor itself, providing drainage channels at the foot of the ballast. Color the rock to match surrounding rock outside the tunnel area, except that you can make it darker and darker as you go inside so as to exaggerate the effect of tunnel depth. This completes the floorwork.

Place a piece of plastic wrapping tissue over the floor and track so that it clings to the floor surface. This is to prevent the next work from spattering the track or floor. See fig. 9-20.

Place pieces of wallboard or any other suitable material over the track to make a core as wide and as high and in the general shaping of the desired tunnel bore. The idea is to cast a tunnel liner over this — but don't do it yet. First wrinkle some heavy aluminum foil and lay it over the core, coming down just to the floor on each side. See fig. 9-21. This wrinkling will simulate the roughness of blasted rock

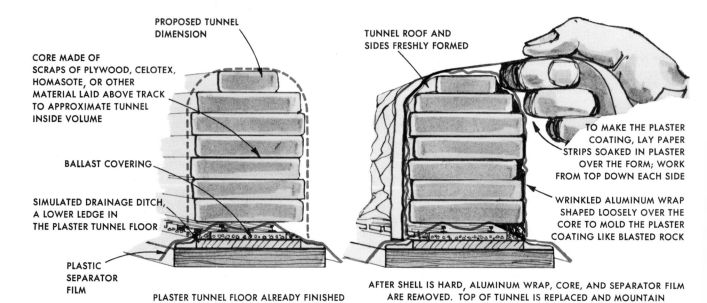

PROPOSED TUNNEL DIMENSION

CORE MADE OF
SCRAPS OF PLYWOOD, CELOTEX,
HOMASOTE, OR OTHER
MATERIAL LAID ABOVE TRACK
TO APPROXIMATE TUNNEL
INSIDE VOLUME

BALLAST COVERING

SIMULATED DRAINAGE DITCH,
A LOWER LEDGE IN
THE PLASTER TUNNEL FLOOR

PLASTIC
SEPARATOR
FILM

PLASTER TUNNEL FLOOR ALREADY FINISHED
AND NOW PROTECTED BY SEPARATOR FILM

TUNNEL ROOF AND
SIDES FRESHLY FORMED

TO MAKE THE PLASTER
COATING, LAY PAPER
STRIPS SOAKED IN PLASTER
OVER THE FORM; WORK
FROM TOP DOWN EACH SIDE

WRINKLED ALUMINUM WRAP
SHAPED LOOSELY OVER THE
CORE TO MOLD THE PLASTER
COATING LIKE BLASTED ROCK

AFTER SHELL IS HARD, ALUMINUM WRAP, CORE, AND SEPARATOR FILM
ARE REMOVED. TOP OF TUNNEL IS REPLACED AND MOUNTAIN
ROCKWORK IS BROUGHT TO JOIN AT THE PORTALS

9-20 Built-up tunnel core.

9-21 Hard shell forms the tunnel walls.

inside the tunnel. Coat the aluminum with something that plaster won't stick to, such as lacquer or melted vegetable shortening.

As an alternative, a rubber mold of a suitable rock surface can be laid rough side up over this core, like a saddle.

Over this form, lay strips of paper towel soaked in plaster the consistency of pancake batter. Work from the roof down each side to the floor. When the first coat is hard, put on another coat this same way. However, to obtain extra strength with this second coat, either use Hydrocal instead of molding plaster, or use rags instead of paper towels with the molding plaster. (Don't use Hydrocal for that first coat, as it doesn't take dye and other penetrating coloring as well as molding plaster.)

In an hour the second coat will be hard, and you can lift the liner, remove the core and form, and color the tunnel roof and walls the same as you did the floor. When you replace the liner, tie it to the floor by wrapping two or three loops of masking tape around the liner, floor, and roadbed: like a man with a toothache in the funnies. This will hold the liner in place firmly, but a slice with a model knife at floor level will free the liner later for any reason, such as repairing track. (With hard shell it is also easy to remove the mountain above the liner and replace it after track repairs; so while this may sound a little revolutionary to those who have not yet tried it, hiding track in a tunnel is no

longer the serious maintenance matter it used to be.)

At the site of the tunnel portal, again stuff the core and form material just inside the existing liner. Then bring the mountain terrain down to the portal area, touching the form of aluminum or rubber. After the plaster is no longer tacky but is still soft, fold the form up and to the sides to impress some of its rock texture into the terrain. A small amount of handwork will remove any traces of artifice. Color the portal and add bits of grass and foliage at appropriate places.

Often the approach to a rock tunnel is where the railroad route suddenly meets a wall of rock: for instance, when threading the canyon of a mountain stream. But in some situations, such as in rolling country, the railroad may penetrate a hill of earth or gravel in a cut for some distance before rock and the need for the tunnel is met.

An interesting bit of detail that is suitable for all but the most modern or very oldest railroads is the telltale. A telltale is simply a warning device; it usually consists of a series of small ropes hanging from a support across the track. These telltales are usually placed about 200 feet or so from the tunnel portal. They are also used in the approach to truss bridges and any other structure where clearance above cars is less than the height of a man. Today men don't ride the tops of trains; but in the days when they did, the dangling ropes of the telltale would brush against any trainman who happened to be standing on top

of a car, warning him to duck if he didn't want to be swept off the top of the train by the roof of the tunnel.

These telltales are easy to make, as shown in fig. 9-22. The framework can be made of ⅛" x ⅛" stripwood in HO; ¼" x ¼" in O scale. The "rope" network hanging from this support can be modeled from screen wire as shown in the illustration.

The width of the framework supporting the telltale depends upon whether it is a single track or multiple tracks approaching the tunnel. I doubt if there was a standard dimension for a telltale support in the prototype, since most of these devices varied in design from road to road to suit the particular styles and whims of each railroad and the clearances of the tunnels. Some were supported by a single upright post that can be made of either metal or timber. Probably the most common type was that supported by a post on either side of the track. These posts should be set far enough to the side of the rails to provide ample clearance for the cars and men on ladders on the sides of cars.

A safe rule to observe is the clearance table as set down by the National Model Railroad Association. If the framework supporting the telltale is on straight track, its minimum width should be 4" (actual) in O scale, 2²⁶⁄₃₂" in S, 2" in HO, and from ²⁶⁄₃₂" to 1" in TT gauge. N scale standards for U. S. practice have not been established as this is written. If the support is placed on a curve, these distances should be widened (according to the

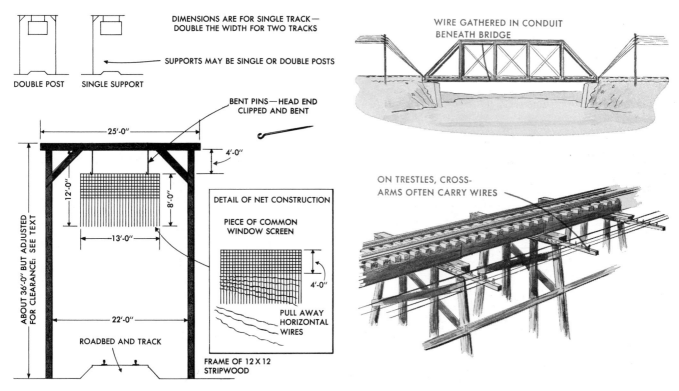

9-22 **Telltale on the Texas & Rio Grande Western.**

9-23 **Telegraph wires at bridges.**

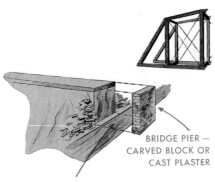

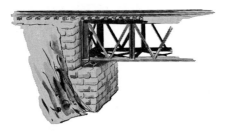

BRIDGE PIER —
CARVED BLOCK OR
CAST PLASTER

CEMENT OR SCREW TO
TRACK SUPPORT BENCHWORK

9-24 Masonry or brick bridge abutment.

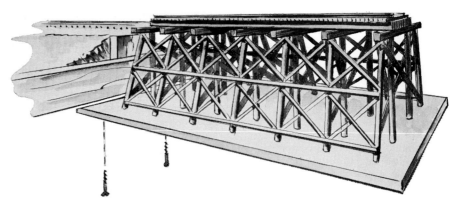

9-25 Trestles can be built easily either at the location or on the workbench if mounted on a flat board. Piles may fit in drilled holes or merely be glued in place.

radius of the curve) to provide ample clearance for all equipment swinging wide on the curve.

The prototype telltale was designed so the rope ends came to a level well below the elevation of the tunnel roof or bridge beams. On a model railroad the bottom of the telltale network hanging from the support should clear the tallest bit of equipment (either locomotive or wrecking crane) which will operate over the track. This clearance is about 5½″ in O scale, 4⅛″ in S, 3″ in HO, 2⅛″ in TT, and 1⅝″ in N scale.

The network can be made by unraveling the lower two thirds of horizontal wires from a rectangular piece of screen.

Telephone and other poles along the track are other details that should not be overlooked in detailing the scenery. As a general rule, these poles

follow alongside the right-of-way fence on one or both sides of the track. However, in some cases where the terrain makes this impossible, as in mountainous country, it is entirely in good taste to allow the line of poles to wander away from the track and follow a course over the mountain. This is especially true where the track runs along a narrow ledge and there is not enough room for both track and poles.

The distance between telephone poles alongside the track varies according to type and height of pole. Some poles on smaller railroad lines have no crossarms at all, but support the wires on insulators attached directly to the tops of the poles. Others may have only one crossarm; others, two or several, depending upon the number of wires to be supported. Probably the most attractive is the two-arm pole with each arm carrying six insulators. These poles should be placed no more than 100 scale feet apart. The simplest way to set the poles in place is to drill a hole in the plaster or roadbed support for a press-fit for the base of the pole.

Telephone poles can be purchased ready-made at the hobby shop, either in kit form or already assembled, or

they can be made from scratch. Medical swab sticks about ⅟₁₆″ in diameter make excellent poles for HO scale and ⅟₃₂″ x ⅟₁₆″ stripwood can be cut to form the crossarms. In the larger gauges, ¼″ doweling and ⅟₁₆″ x ⅛″ stripwood can be used. Height of the poles varies, but a good standard dimension to use is 30 scale feet above ground.

Some modelers go to the extreme of stringing actual wires on their poles, using either fine magnet wire or silk thread. The chief trouble is that this maze of wire network eventually turns into a very efficient air filter and catches all the dust that drifts over the model railroad. Also, such wiring is a great handicap to proper layout maintenance.

What happens to the telephone and telegraph wires when the lines come to a wide crossing such as a river or deep canyon? Two of the simplest solutions (on the prototype) to this problem are shown in fig. 9-23:

● The wires run down from the pole at either end of the bridge into a conduit which in turn is strung along underneath the bridge.

● The wires are carried on crossarms affixed to the bridge or trestle structure.

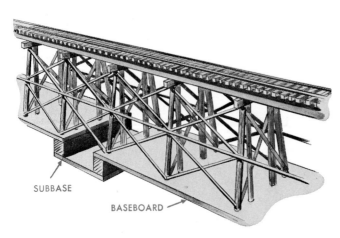

SUBBASE

BASEBOARD

9-26 Mounting board may have a gap closed by subbase if a deep stream passes under at one point. Be sure joints are rigid. Same idea can provide for a low-level track or highway.

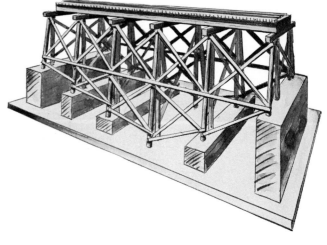

9-27 In rugged terrain, bents of varied height may be supported on blocks. See also Fig. 9-28 at right.

BRIDGE and trestle piers and trestle foundations also are scenery details that can be built or set in place as an integral part of the original plaster and should be constructed or at least planned when putting in the basic scenery. Bridge piers may be of several different types of construction, depending upon the type of bridge to be supported. Actually bridge piers serve two purposes. Most important, of course, is the function of supporting the bridge itself. Second, the pier serves as a sort of retaining wall to prevent the earth and rock from eroding under the track at either end of the bridge.

If the bridge is to be a fairly modern one and extremely heavy, it can be held up by concrete piers. Older large bridges can be supported on stone or some other form of masonry. Lighter bridges and trestles can have a cribbing foundation made of heavy timbers. In some instances, a bent of heavy timbers is driven into the earth at the trestle end and a retaining wall made of heavy timbers is constructed between the bent and the earth bank.

The modern bridge pier of concrete, like the modern tunnel portal, may range from a single, very plain, heavy block of concrete to an elaborately built affair with many ledges and ornamental rectangular columns and arches. Photographs of the prototype, such as are found in TRAINS magazine, are a fine guide in selecting the type of bridge pier.

On my layout there are 13 bridges and trestles ranging from a modern double-track steel truss bridge 315 scale feet long to an old wooden-beam truss bridge. The piers supporting them range from old stone to modern concrete — and all were made the same way, from blocks of soft pine sawed to the proper shape and painted, then screwed or cemented in place as shown in fig. 9-24.

Since the bents of an old wooden trestle rest on, or in, the earth, it is obvious that this type of structure must be built in advance, or at least

along with, the surrounding scenery. Trestles may be built of wood, reinforced concrete, or steel. They differ from the bridge in that they have supports at regular intervals beneath them for their entire length, whereas a bridge is supported only at each end.

Wood trestles are by far the most picturesque modelwise. In the prototype, wood trestles are generally used for semipermanent work, or where their first cost is less than an earth fill or earth fill and culvert, if a stream is to be crossed. Frequently a fill would be cheaper than a trestle, but less practical. This is especially true in bridging a swiftly flowing stream which floods after heavy rains, causing a swift flow of water.

From the scenic standpoint, it should be noted that the ground beneath a trestle on most well-regulated roads is kept clear of brush and weeds as a means of fire prevention. Without going into the detail of trestle construction, I think it wise to outline some of the problems that go with setting such a structure in place in the model scene.

If the trestle is to cross an almost-level stretch of ground, and all the supporting bents are the same height, the matter is simple, as shown in fig. 9-25. Build the trestle on a flat piece of board as shown and set it in place. Plaster can be worked around the bases of the bents and a few pebbles can be embedded in it to give a rocky effect. The trestle that crosses uneven and slanting ground is much more attractive than the monotonous trestle which has all its bents exactly the same height, but its installation is more complex.

Trestles crossing uneven earth will naturally have supporting bents of different heights. This means they cannot all rest on an even flat surface such as was used in the type of construction just described; yet these bents must rest firmly on something to give them support. This problem can be solved by building the entire structure on a flat piece of wood, but

Clint Grant.

9-29 Details such as bumpers, stone railings, gardens, a fountain, and lampposts were added at the terminal of my Texas & Rio Grande Western.

filling in under the shorter bents with blocks of wood tacked, screwed, or cemented to the flat subbase of wood (fig. 9-27). The screen or wadded paper for hard-shell support is then leveled along the tops of these blocks, creating a slanting or a rough and rugged terrain beneath the trestle. See fig. 9-28.

Trestle construction differs according to the earth over which it is built. If the ground underneath is yielding enough, the timbers forming the supporting bents are sometimes driven into the earth with pile drivers. Ground which is yielding enough to permit this type of construction will not lie at an angle of more than 30 degrees from the horizontal. This type of construction is called a "pile bent." In many cases the earth is too rocky or too steeply sloped to permit this type of trestle construction: then the bents will rest on foundations. These foundations may be wood subsills or cribs, or stone or concrete piers. This type of construction is then called a "framed bent."

Space does not permit us to go into detail at this time on trestle construction, but for those interested in that type of construction I recommend the book by Paul Mallery, *Bridge & Trestle Handbook for Model Railroaders*. The NMRA Data Sheets from D6b through D6b.4 also give valuable information on trestles and their foundations.

To conclude this chapter on details, here are a few little tricks that the old-timers use to gain depth and perspective in their scenery. If you already are aware of these tricks, consider yourself an old-timer.

Place the larger, full-size detail nearest the spectators' areas; then gradually diminish the size of the detail toward the rear of the layout. This applies to buildings, trees, shrubs, and other objects which would naturally shrink in size in the distance to

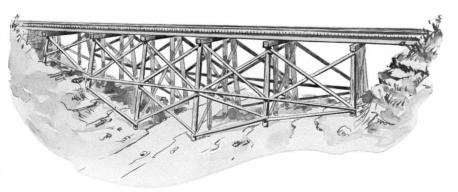

9-28 Screen is tacked to supporting board and blocks. Then plaster is worked up to base of each trestle bent and finished so trestle appears to have earth supporting it.

the observer's eye. The distance from front to rear on most model railroads is so short that objects in the scene don't have a chance to assume the natural perspective, so we sort of force perspective on them to heighten the illusion of distance by allowing structures and trees to shrink as they get farther away from the eye.

Another trick popular with most mystic knights of the model rail is that of underscaling all man-made structures, even those in the immediate foreground. For instance, I know of many HO gaugers who build all rolling stock, locomotives, etc., to the standard 3.5 mm. scale — but in building their structures, they stick to a ⅛"-to-the-foot scale. Even in building their railroad structures, such as a trestle, they purposely fudge a little on the scale timbers. For instance, if plans call for a 100-foot trestle built with timber bents made of 12 x 12 timbers, said trestle is built to 100 scale feet using the 3.5 mm. scale for the overall size. But in selecting the stripwood for the construction, instead of using wood 3.5 mm. square to represent the 12 x 12 timbers, the builder drops about 10 percent and uses a piece of stripwood ⅛" square. This gives the trestle a finer, more spiderweb effect, but hardly perceptible as undersize.

However, in the case of structures such as stations, freight houses, and other buildings found in the immediate foreground, not only reduce the scale size of the lumber used, but also reduce the overall scale of the building to ⅛". These smaller structures tend to make the layout look larger and the rolling equipment more massive.

Care should be exercised in the placement of buildings anywhere near mountains that are supposed to represent towering peaks. For instance, the effect of a mountain range in the background is spoiled entirely if there is a 10-story building taller than the mountain range directly in front of it. It would be more effective if all buildings in front of the range were confined to one story (two at the most). If the mountains are far enough back on the layout so that they appear to be far in the distance, the taller buildings can be used. But if there are only a few feet separating the skyscrapers from the mountains, keep your buildings low and squatty.

A. L. Schmidt.

10 BLENDING BACKGROUND SCENERY

Baltimore & Ohio R.R.

10-1 Larry Sagle at the B&O HO exhibit.

EVEN the most marvelously created and realistic third-dimensional scenery will be all the more effective if you add a scenic backdrop to lend the feeling of great distances to the modeling. On the other hand, good scenery loses much of its effectiveness if the wall beyond is cluttered with anything that distracts the eye and does not blend in with the scenery in the immediate foreground. Such things as windows, pipes, pictures on the wall, shelves, and calendars can be particularly distracting when they loom beyond your railroad.

Backdrops are usually used only when the railroad is built on a shelf next to, or at least near, the walls of the room. But before we get into the general discussion, let's consider the "island railroad," built on a table you walk around. With this type of railroad, anything that is put on the wall in the form of a scenic backdrop is so far beyond the opposite side of the table that it cannot blend into the modeled scenery directly.

One of the best solutions for a backdrop behind an island layout is a curtain of some sort in a solid hue, possibly a powder or sky blue, or a neutral gray, hung on the wall to hide all objects which might cause the eye to wander away from the center of attraction, the railroad itself.

Sometimes you can install a two-sided backdrop right down the center of a table. If you have the book *101 Track Plans*, look at plan no. 87 for a good example of this idea. John Armstrong also used this idea on his home railroad in Silver Spring, Maryland, and in some of his track plans.

When your railroad is built against a wall or only a short distance in front of it, a scenic background of one sort or another becomes very important. If there is enough space between the last visible tracks *nearest* the wall and the wall itself, this void can be filled by building 3-D scenery almost as high as the ceiling itself — that is, if you are modeling mountainous country. The remaining space between the tops of these mountains, which should be above eye level, and the ceiling could be covered with a plain blue backdrop representing blue sky.

But most model railroaders are either so cramped for space, or want to utilize every spare inch of space for trackwork, that they lay their rails only a few inches away from the wall. This leaves only a narrow strip along the back side of the layout which can be scenicked, and they must use a painted or printed backdrop similar to those used in the old vaudeville theaters.

The average railroader has three sources of backdrops to choose from:

● He can buy a printed backdrop from the hobby shop.

● He can paint his own mural — or hire it done by a good-natured artist friend.

● He can use photomurals.

There is one other possible source — large printed advertising posters which are used in window displays by the local drug or grocery stores. However, the modeler could take a full course in oil painting and create his own background in the time it would take to find a printed landscape that has everything in the background in proper scale and in a color that would not clash with his scenery.

That is one important angle that the builder must take into consideration in selection of his backdrop, regardless of whether it is something the village merchant is throwing away or whether it is a purchased, printed hobby shop backdrop or a photomural from the local Kodak clicker. The scenery in the backdrop must be akin to the type depicted on the layout itself. If you are modeling the Arizona desert, obviously it would *not* be in keeping to hang a backdrop in the rear which depicts the cool, green, rolling hills of Maryland or Kentucky.

I recall once having seen photos of an early-day model railroad in which the scenery was well done. In the background was hung an advertising poster scrounged from the village merchant's store. The layout was beautifully done in HO scale; the buildings depicting a station scene and allied industries and engine servicing facilities were well done and to proper proportion. All in all it gave a striking effect — as long as your eyes didn't wander to the background.

But that background! First of all, it seemed to be of a semitropical scene entirely out of harmony with the type of foliage in the foreground. And right smack-dab in the middle was a building of Spanish or possibly Italian architecture with a balcony such as might have been used by Romeo and Juliet. And the whole thing — building, trees, and all—was done in a scale that would have been large even if the railroad had been done in 1″-to-the-foot scale. The balcony alone was larger than the entire railroad station beside the track. And it was in the perspective that you might get had you been viewing it from the mouth of a nearby storm cellar — looking up at it. All the while you were looking *down* on top of the roofs of the buildings on the layout proper.

So, in selection of a backdrop, whether it be a photomural, a painting, or a purchased lithographed or painted scene, the most important thing to consider is whether it is in correct scale and proportion to the scenes on the layout. Another important angle to consider is the lighting effect of the background. Backdrops blend in with the layout best if they are painted or photographed in *flat* lighting conditions and show *no deep shadows*. For those unfamiliar with the techniques involved in photographing or painting a landscape in "flat lighting" — let me try to explain the term.

On a bright, sunshiny day, trees, buildings, posts, and other objects which rise above ground level cast a shadow, the length of which depends upon the time of day. These shadows point away from the sun. "Flat lighting" is that type of light we encounter on a day when it is cloudy or when there is a high overcast. There are no deep shadows extending from the bases of buildings, trees or posts — or people. Admittedly, this concern with lighting in the background may be a minor technicality, but it is a point

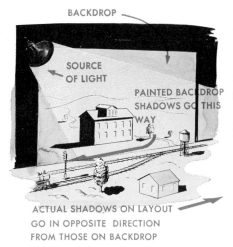

BACKDROP

SOURCE
OF LIGHT

PAINTED BACKDROP
SHADOWS GO THIS
WAY

ACTUAL SHADOWS ON LAYOUT
GO IN OPPOSITE DIRECTION
FROM THOSE ON BACKDROP

10-2 Avoid shadows in the foreground that don't match shadows in the backdrop.

worth considering in the selection of a backdrop.

For instance, let us say that you select a backdrop painted or photographed in bright light and the shadows from the bases of buildings and trees extend to the LEFT. Now, against this background, let us say your layout is lighted from the LEFT-HAND SIDE; then the actual shadows on your 3-D scenery will extend from the bases of your buildings and trees to the RIGHT (fig. 10-2) — obviously an impossible situation, as the sun doesn't cast shadows in two directions at once.

The absence of shadows on a backdrop painted to simulate flat lighting is not nearly so noticeable as having wrong shadows. If someone does discover this inconsistency you put your tongue in cheek and explain:

It is a partly cloudy day and the section of the layout casting shadows is bathed in sunlight, but the broken clouds are over the section represented in the flat-lighted backdrop. Hence, no shadows.

Incidentally, this problem of lighting the 3-D portions of the scenery — the plaster hills, cuts, and fills — is of major importance. Poor illumination can kill the effect of even the best of scenery, while excellent, realistic lighting can enhance scenery of poor quality.

In the art galleries, a great deal of attention is paid to the proper lighting of the old masters hung on the wall. We model railroaders are artists in the sense that we are creating scenes in three dimensions. It is just as important — even more so — that our creations be properly lighted to get the best effect.

The Wizard of Monterey, John Allen, once illustrated this problem to me graphically by the use of some color slides of his fabulous Gorre & Daphetid RR. He first showed some slides of scenes made on his railroad under proper lighting conditions. The realism and beauty of the rugged mountain country was breathtaking. Then he displayed slides of the same scenes, taken by the same camera from the same angles, but improperly lighted. The same scenes which had appeared so realistic under proper lighting looked artificial.

Later, John visited my attic Texas & Rio Grande Western system. I had told John in advance that proper lighting was my number one scenic problem. After taking a quick look around the layout, John agreed. He suggested I experiment with lighting from different angles.

I tried using a portable photoflood spotlight stand with a common 100-watt household bulb instead of the photoflood bulb. (The photoflood bulb is okay for taking photographs, but is too brilliant for the naked eye.) I experimented with John's suggestions, moving the floodlight from point to point, altering the angle and height from which the light source shone upon the scenery, and was amazed at the different results. Scenes that appeared dull and drab and lifeless under ordinary center ceiling lights in the attic snapped out and became more realistic.

Now, like all scenery problems, lighting is an individual one. It is practically impossible to set down any hard and fast rules for correct illumination that will apply to all layouts. The type of lighting that may show Joe Doakes's railroad to its best advantage may make John Q. Blow's layout look like the town junkyard. The best way to find the answer to this one is to fall back on the old solution — EXPERIMENT — with a portable light source.

One of the most effective methods of lighting the layout, especially if it is an around-the-wall railroad (that is, the tablework supporting the tracks circles the room adjoining the wall), is valance lighting. With this type of lighting, a curtain or valance about a foot deep runs the length of each wall; it hangs from the ceiling and conceals the light bulbs, reflecting a sort of flat light on the layout itself. Fig. 10-3 illustrates this type of lighting. There is no end of tricks that can be performed with valance lighting. Valance lighting is a form of stage footlight illumination; the difference is that stage footlights shine upward, while valance lighting throws the illumination downward.

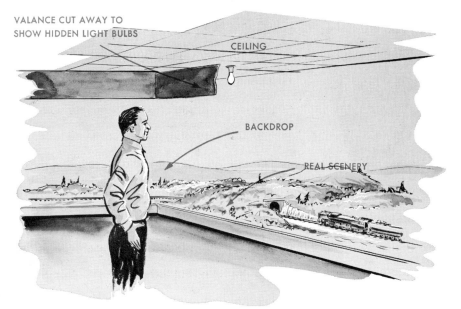

VALANCE CUT AWAY TO
SHOW HIDDEN LIGHT BULBS

CEILING

BACKDROP

REAL SCENERY

10-3 Valance hides lights from eyes.

VALANCE TOO LOW

HALF OF LAYOUT HIDDEN
BY VALANCE

LINE OF VISION

WALL

CROSS SECTION
OF LAYOUT

10-4 Valance too low also hides scenery.

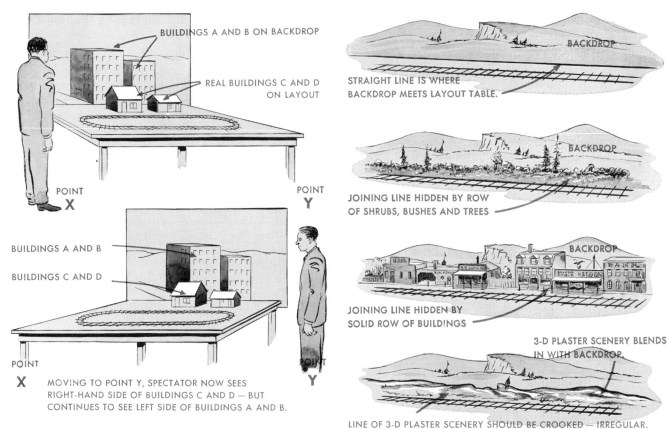

BUILDINGS A AND B ON BACKDROP

REAL BUILDINGS C AND D ON LAYOUT

POINT X   POINT Y

BUILDINGS A AND B

BUILDINGS C AND D

POINT X   POINT Y

MOVING TO POINT Y, SPECTATOR NOW SEES RIGHT-HAND SIDE OF BUILDINGS C AND D — BUT CONTINUES TO SEE LEFT SIDE OF BUILDINGS A AND B.

STRAIGHT LINE IS WHERE BACKDROP MEETS LAYOUT TABLE.

JOINING LINE HIDDEN BY ROW OF SHRUBS, BUSHES AND TREES

JOINING LINE HIDDEN BY SOLID ROW OF BUILDINGS

3-D PLASTER SCENERY BLENDS IN WITH BACKDROP.

LINE OF 3-D PLASTER SCENERY SHOULD BE CROOKED — IRREGULAR.

10-5 Background perspective doesn't change, but foreground does as you move about to different points of view.

10-6 Try to hide joint made by the backdrop painting.

By alternating different colored bulbs connected to separate circuits back of the valance, the operator can run the gamut of lighting effects on his railroad. Warm, orange-colored bulbs all connected on the same circuit can simulate the early morning glow of the rising sun. The stronger, more brilliant white lights will give the effect of midday sun. Then the operator can switch back to the orange bulbs for the effect of late afternoon and the setting sun. Blue bulbs give a moonlight effect if used sparingly. Some railroaders have been known to hook up this type of lighting to an automatic device which is constantly changing the intensity of the illumination. This gives a striking, realistic effect.

Valance lighting is not adaptable to all railroads — more especially, those built in an attic room with sloping ceilings. The lower edge of the valance should not be lower than eye level; otherwise it might hide part of the railroad, as illustrated in fig. 10-4. Anyone seriously considering valance lighting should first make sure the electrical circuits to his railroad room are adequate to carry the added load of this type of illumination.

Now, back to the subject of backdrops. I personally try to avoid any backdrops that include buildings painted in perspective. The reason for this is that the perspective of all three-dimensional objects is different from every viewing angle, while that of a painted geometric object on the backdrop cannot change. As you move about the room the frozen pattern of the backdrop buildings is very noticeable.

To better illustrate this point, let us study fig. 10-5. There are two buildings, A and B, painted in perspective on the backdrop. Structures C and D are kitbuilt (or scratchbuilt) buildings on the layout. Now, as long as you view the scene from point X, all buildings are in about the same perspective. You see the left-hand sides of all buildings, the real ones and the painted ones. But when you move over to point Y, you see the right-hand sides of buildings C and D (the real ones), but you continue to see the left side only of the painted buildings A and B. Moving up and down is just as serious. Like the conflicting shadows, this point may be minor and highly technical, but it is one of the little details that contribute toward making the scene more realistic.

If you feel you *must* have some buildings in your backdrop, then paint them first. Show one side only: the side nearest you. It is a good idea to keep them as far in the background as possible; the farther you are away from a structure, the less the perspective changes.

Earlier in this chapter, mention was made of photomurals as backdrops. I've seen some very realistic pikes with large photos as a background. Cliff Robinson, an old-timer in the hobby, used a photomural of the Dallas skyline as a backdrop for his Marquette Union Terminal RR., and it was quite effective. Oddly enough, the perspective of the skyscrapers and other buildings is held to a minimum and is not as noticeable as in a painting or drawing. This may be due to the fact that the camera taking the mural may have been swung in an arc to get a panorama effect from a fixed point, and the entire shot shows the buildings at a distance.

Photomurals are expensive, especially if they are done in full color. A sepia-toned photomural is highly preferable to an ordinary black-and-white photo; the toning seems to blend better with the more vivid colors of the layout. However, if you have a black-and-white — or even a sepia-toned — photomural, and want it in colors, and if you are willing to spend a little time at the task, it can be converted into a full-color job. Both watercolor and oil paints especially prepared for tinting black-and-white photos are available at most well-equipped camera stores.

In tinting the background photomural, as well as in painting and creating your own backdrop from a drawing, it should be remembered that nature's colors fade in intensity with distance. A mountain that may be heavily studded with deep-green pines when viewed from its base gradually fades to a misty blue the farther we drive away from it.

Pikes Peak, the pride and joy of Colorado, is actually a jumble of brown, tan, and red rocks above timber line, but the top appears to be a light brown when viewed from the base at Manitou Springs or from Colorado Springs. When you get your first sight of it as you approach from many miles away, it appears to be a slate blue.

Let us suppose you have solved the backdrop problem to your satisfaction and have the painting or photo in place. Now comes the problem of blending it into the three-dimensional foreground and midground of the layout scenery. Where the backdrop meets the table edge there is a straight line. Now, there are no straight lines in nature, except perhaps for the horizon line on the sea or a very flat plain, and that line is at eye level. This one isn't. The eyes of the spectator observing the layout rove easily across the scene, from the trackwork nearest him, over the hills, through the ravines and creeks — until they hit that straight line of the table edge joining the background. There they receive a jolt, like an automobile tire hitting a sharp bump in the road.

We want to eliminate that straight line and provide a bridge for the eye from actual scenery to the fake backdrop. This can be done in a number of ways — principally by:

● Hiding the straight line with an uneven row of trees and shrubbery at the edge of the table.

● Placing a row of buildings in front of the backdrop. (Sure, you'll have a straight line where the buildings rest on the layout-table street — but that is man-made scenery, and there are plenty of straight lines in structures.)

● Placing a bit of liftout — or it can be permanent — scenery depicting a low, rocky ridge between the farthest track and the edge of the table. These three solutions are shown in fig. 10-6.

One major problem that occurs in blending the actual scenery with that in the backdrop is that posed by rivers or highways which flow away from the spectator *into* the painted backdrop. Let's take a river as an example, as shown in fig. 10-8. It twists and winds through the plaster banks of the real scenery on the layout until it meets the flat painted or photographed backdrop. WHAM! There's that straight line of the joint between the table and the backdrop.

The solution? Simply let the stream

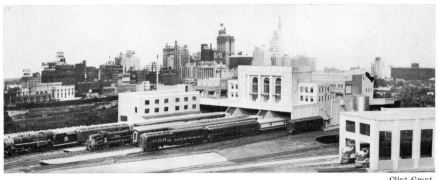

Clint Grant.

10-7 **Cliff Robinson used a photo panorama of Dallas behind his terminal.**

get lost behind a clump of trees and shrubs — or behind a rocky promontory. Then it reappears on the background scenery apparently winding out from behind this obstructing hill or clump of shrubs. A highway or road can rise over the brow of a plaster hill, dropping off on the other side; then it appears or picks up on the painted backdrop after taking a sharp dip which is hidden by the brow of the hill.

This business of blending the background and the layout scenery can be cleverly done. I have seen countless photos in the model railroad magazines where it is impossible to tell where the real scenery ends and the flat, painted landscape begins.

Actually, there are two schools of conflicting thought as to whether the real third-dimensional scenery should ever *touch* the painted backdrop. One school contends that there should always be at least an inch or two between the rugged edge of the real scenery and the backdrop; some con-

tend that there can be as much as 15 or 20 inches of space between the two without losing the effect. The other school contends that it is entirely more realistic to bring plaster, trees and shrubbery right up to, and join, the backdrop.

There is one nationally recognized authority on scenery who paints clumps of trees on his backdrop, then *cements* actual scale model trees across the face of these painted trees. After he has fastened the backdrop in place, he plants more trees in the plaster scenery in front of this combination. In the resulting scene, it is impossible to tell where the real scale model trees end and where the painted trees start. This same expert also has been known to attach his plaster mountains directly to the backdrop, following a method similar to that shown in fig. 10-10.

I've always gone along with the first school of thought — that is, the background should never touch the foreground physically. However, after

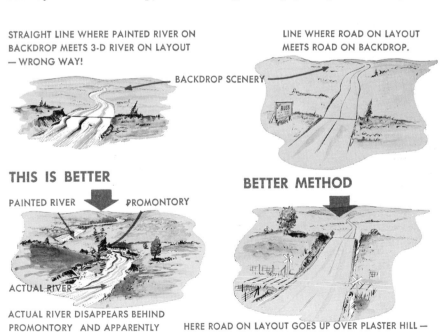

STRAIGHT LINE WHERE PAINTED RIVER ON BACKDROP MEETS 3-D RIVER ON LAYOUT — WRONG WAY!

LINE WHERE ROAD ON LAYOUT MEETS ROAD ON BACKDROP.

BACKDROP SCENERY

THIS IS BETTER

PAINTED RIVER   PROMONTORY

ACTUAL RIVER

BETTER METHOD

ACTUAL RIVER DISAPPEARS BEHIND PROMONTORY AND APPARENTLY CONTINUES ON IN PAINTED BACKDROP — NO STRAIGHT LINE.

HERE ROAD ON LAYOUT GOES UP OVER PLASTER HILL — APPARENTLY DROPS OFF ON OTHER SIDE INTO SHARP DIP — THEN RISES AGAIN ON BACKDROP SCENE.

10-8 **Tricks for backdrop joint blending.**

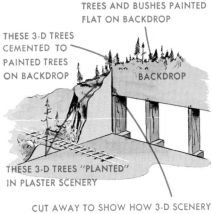

THESE 3-D TREES CEMENTED TO PAINTED TREES ON BACKDROP

TREES AND BUSHES PAINTED FLAT ON BACKDROP

BACKDROP

THESE 3-D TREES "PLANTED" IN PLASTER SCENERY

CUT AWAY TO SHOW HOW 3-D SCENERY ACTUALLY TOUCHES BACKDROP

10-9 Paint trees slightly smaller on backdrop so they blend with model trees.

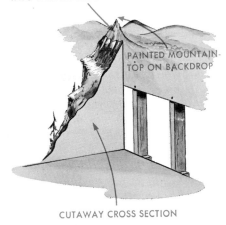

PLASTER OF MOUNTAIN JOINS AND BLENDS INTO PAINTED MOUNTAINTOP ON BACKDROP

PAINTED MOUNTAINTOP ON BACKDROP

CUTAWAY CROSS SECTION

10-10 Edge of plaster follows profile.

All photos, Clint Grant.

10-12 These photos show steps in adding a bas-relief background to form a transition between the fully modeled foreground and the flat painted backdrop. Wall is first painted a plain color. Foreground mountain and track scenes are modeled, leaving just 2″ or 3″ of space at rear for bas-relief. Backdrop scene is then painted on wall. Next, bas-relief, which has been modeled on shallow upright screen and frame, is completed and then set in place between them.

seeing some of the results the other side gets, I'm convinced either method is good. It's just another case of using the method with which you personally get the most realistic results.

A few paragraphs back, I mentioned that one way of blending the actual scene with the landscaped backdrop is to place a row of buildings along the back edge of the table, between

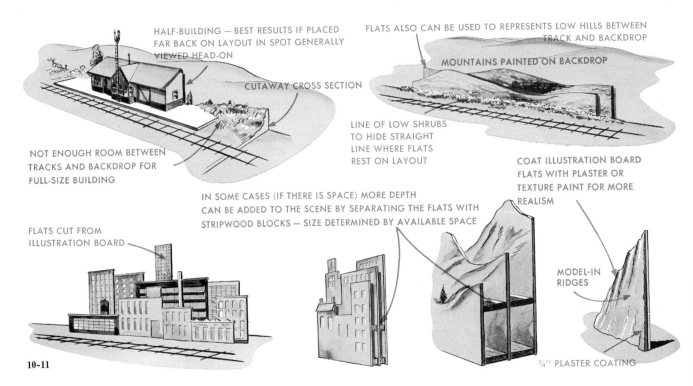

HALF-BUILDING — BEST RESULTS IF PLACED FAR BACK ON LAYOUT IN SPOT GENERALLY VIEWED HEAD-ON

CUTAWAY CROSS SECTION

NOT ENOUGH ROOM BETWEEN TRACKS AND BACKDROP FOR FULL-SIZE BUILDING

FLATS ALSO CAN BE USED TO REPRESENTS LOW HILLS BETWEEN TRACK AND BACKDROP

MOUNTAINS PAINTED ON BACKDROP

LINE OF LOW SHRUBS TO HIDE STRAIGHT LINE WHERE FLATS REST ON LAYOUT

COAT ILLUSTRATION BOARD FLATS WITH PLASTER OR TEXTURE PAINT FOR MORE REALISM

IN SOME CASES (IF THERE IS SPACE) MORE DEPTH CAN BE ADDED TO THE SCENE BY SEPARATING THE FLATS WITH STRIPWOOD BLOCKS — SIZE DETERMINED BY AVAILABLE SPACE

FLATS CUT FROM ILLUSTRATION BOARD

MODEL-IN RIDGES

¼″ PLASTER COATING

10-11

102

the actual scenery on the layout table and the backdrop. There are several ways of doing this. If there is room, several inches or more, it is possible to place a complete building with all four sides in this area. But if there is only 2″ or 3″ between the tracks and the backdrop, a "half-building" or a series of cutout flats properly staggered will give remarkable results. See fig. 10-11.

Earl Cochran had one of these half-buildings, a combination station, on his famous Ute Short Line in Colorado Springs. It was located high in the mountains at the back side of the layout, in a space about 2½″ wide between the tracks and the background scenery. When viewed from the front of the layout it was impossible to tell the difference between it and a fully constructed station.

Cochran, like Ellison, also used cutout flats of buildings staggered realistically to give the effect of a distant town's skyline. These flats should be made of a good, heavy grade of artist's illustration board. It is a good idea to brace them in the rear by cementing stripwood from top to bottom to keep them from warping. Cliff Robinson also has made effective use of half-buildings on his layout, as shown in fig. 10-7.

You can design your own buildings, or copy photos and drawings in magazines. Windows can be either cut out or painted on the flats; it's just according to how much trouble you want to take with the things. In case you decide to go first class and cut out the windows, then the openings should be backed up with clear plastic to represent the glass. Cover half of this backing with strips of green paper or ribbon to represent curtains. In the case of flats that are placed far back on the layout, I believe windows drawn in and painted solid black or a deep blue are just as effective as cutout openings.

Not only can flats be used to simulate buildings and form a city skyline in the distance, they can also be used to represent a low range of hills. These flats can be made even more effective by covering them with a layer of texture paint or plaster about ¼″ thick. Stipple the plaster as described in the earlier part of this book, scribe in erosion lines, and then paint. If you prefer large mountains, it might be better to saw them out of ¼″ plywood and cover them with a layer of stippled plaster.

If you are not afraid of your artistic talent, there is still another method of making a very effective backdrop.

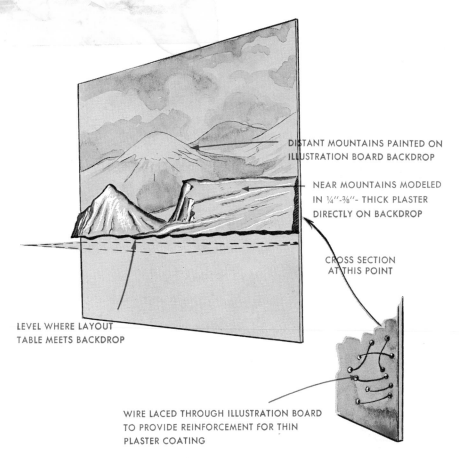

DISTANT MOUNTAINS PAINTED ON ILLUSTRATION BOARD BACKDROP

NEAR MOUNTAINS MODELED IN ¼″-⅜″- THICK PLASTER DIRECTLY ON BACKDROP

CROSS SECTION AT THIS POINT

LEVEL WHERE LAYOUT TABLE MEETS BACKDROP

WIRE LACED THROUGH ILLUSTRATION BOARD TO PROVIDE REINFORCEMENT FOR THIN PLASTER COATING

10-13 Salt-map bas-relief is very thin.

Remember the old "salt maps" you made in geography classes in grammar school to show the locations of mountains and rivers on a continent? They were actually relief maps made on cardboard. The map was first drawn; then the land areas were filled in with a mixture of salt, flour, and water. By lumping it and pinching it at the proper places, it was possible to model a range of mountains in relief.

This same technique could be used to form a three-dimensional backdrop. Use a top grade of the heaviest illustration board. This material can be purchased at art supply stores and the largest size sheet is about 30″ x 40″. If the area to be covered by the backdrop is large, more than one sheet of illustration board may be needed.

Using a mountain scene clipped from a travel magazine as a model, sketch your mountain-range background. Paint the sky a light blue. The most distant mountains should be almost the same shade as the sky — just enough difference in hue to make the mountains stand out from the sky. Mountains in the middle distance should be a bit greener and browner. Finally, the nearest mountains can be given the old "salt map" treatment.

I'd advise that you use plaster instead of flour and salt; it's more durable, and it won't attract visiting cockroaches or mice.

Fill in the outline of the nearest mountains with plaster. It might be a good idea to weave some wire haphazardly into and out of holes in the area to reinforce the plaster and keep it from dropping off if it cracks. Apply the plaster layer no thicker than ¼″ to ⅜″. See fig. 10-13. After it has dried, paint the plaster; or stain it in subdued hues that harmonize with your three-dimensional scenery on the layout.

In winding up this dissertation on scenery, I'd like to call attention to that old saying of the hobby, "Model railroading is something that can't be rushed." This old saw certainly applies as much to the building of scenery as it does to the assembly of engines, cars, and structures. The modeler should devote as much attention to detail and take as much care in building his scenery as he does in all other phases of the hobby. If he does, he will end up with something of which he can be proud, and something that will continue to increase his enjoyment of model railroading.

Easy-to-Build
ELECTRONIC PROJECTS
for Model Railroaders

BY PETER J. THORNE

All the information you need to build your own electronic machine power supplies to steam and diesel sound systems

HOW TO REPAIR COMMERCIAL THROTTLES

Including parts lists, schematics, and step-by-step instructions

Build your own WALKAROUND THROTTLE!

A SPECIAL REPRINT FROM **Model Railroader** MAGAZINE

CTC-16e

A model railroad command control system you can build

BY KEITH GUTIERREZ

The ideal book for beginners!

THE **abc's** OF
from the pages of **Model Railroader**
MODEL RAILROADING

23 chapters to help you get started in model railroading

SCENERY
FOR MODEL RAILROADS

BY BILL McCLANAHAN

REVISED EDITION INCLUDING HARD-SHELL SCENERY AND ZIP TEXTURING

**HOW THE EXPERTS DO IT
MADE EASY FOR BEGINNERS**

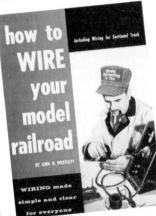

Including Wiring for Sectional Track

how to WIRE your model railroad

BY LINN H. WESTCOTT

WIRING made simple and clear for everyone

HO RAILROAD that grows
By Linn H. Westcott

8 easy steps

Start on a sheet of ply

Including Bridges, Scenery, and Wiring

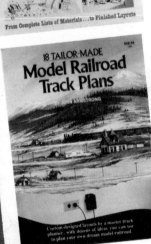

ALL NEW
FUN FOR THE ENTIRE FAMILY

small railroads YOU can build

EDITED BY BOB HAYDEN

Proven Methods Plus NEW Ideas for Scenery, Wiring, Operation

From Complete Lists of Materials...to Finished Layouts

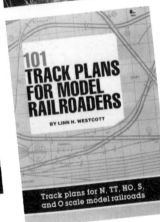

a project railroad from
Model Railroader
HO Narrow Gauge Railroad You Can Build

BY MALCOLM FURLOW

SAN & JUAN CENTRALS

How to Build the San Juan Central — an 8 x 10 HOn3 layout that features sectional construction and new, lightweight scenery techniques

N Scale Primer
A BEGINNER'S GUIDE TO N SCALE MODEL RAILROADING
BY RUSS LARSON

Planning • Carpentry • Trackwork • Wiring • Scenery • Loco

TRACK PLANS FOR SECTIONAL TRACK

By Linn Westcott

144 TRACK PLANS

including lists of pieces needed for rug, table and custom layouts

HO, O-27, S and O gauges

18 TAILOR-MADE
Model Railroad Track Plans

BY JOHN ARMSTRONG

Custom-designed layouts by a master track planner, with dozens of ideas you can use to plan your own dream model railroad

101 TRACK PLANS FOR MODEL RAILROADERS

BY LINN H. WESTCOTT

Track plans for N, TT, HO, S, and O scale model railroads

a project railroad from
Model Railroader
BUILDING AN HO MODEL RAILROAD WITH PERSONALITY

By John Olson

The Jerome & Southwestern: A colorful western layout you can build step by step

A HANDBOOK FOR MODEL RAILROADERS AND
TRACK PLANNING for realistic operation
BY JOHN ARMSTRONG

REVISED AND UPDATED

3373

How prototype railroads are designed to operate

How you can design your model railroad